Private, and not for Publication.]

(769)

Great Western Railway.

RULES

AND

REGULATIONS

FOR THE GUIDANCE

OF THE

OFFICERS AND MEN.

To come into operation on 1st January, 1905.

LONDON:
WATERLOW & SONS LIMITED, PRINTERS, LONDON WALL.
1904.

TABLE OF CONTENTS.

GREAT WESTERN RAILWAY.

Paddington, 1st December, 1904.

The following is a copy of the code of Rules and Regulations for the guidance of all the Officers and Servants of the Company, approved by the Board of Directors on ~~*20th October,*~~ *10th November* 1904, *as per minute printed hereunder.*

JAMES C. INGLIS,

General Manager.

RESOLVED,—

That the existing Book of Rules and Regulations be cancelled and repealed as from the 1st January next, and that the code of Rules and Regulations now submitted be and the same is hereby approved and adopted for regulating the conduct of the Officers and Servants of the Great Western Railway Company on and from the said 1st January next.

That the Common Seal of the Company be affixed to the said code.

That a copy of the said Rules and Regulations be given to every Officer and Servant of the Company affected thereby, and that every such Officer and Servant shall have such copy with him when on duty.

G. K. MILLS,

Secretary.

THESE RULES AND REGULATIONS *have been agreed to generally by the Companies parties to the Railway Clearing System, and apply--subject to modifications which may be made from time to time, due notice of which will be given in the Appendix—to the Great Western Company's Line, whether in respect of their own Engines, Trains, and Servants, or those of other Companies running over their Line. The Servants of the Great Western Railway Company working over the Lines of other Companies will be bound by these Rules and Regulations, and such modifications thereof as may be issued from time to time, except where the owning Company have any exceptional or additional Rules and Regulations, in which case they will be bound by the Rules and Regulations of that Company.*

Every Servant supplied with this Book must make himself thoroughly acquainted with, and will be held responsible for a knowledge of, and compliance with, the whole of the following Rules and Regulations.

DETAILED INDEX.

A.

B.

C.

D.

G.

H.

I.

J.

L.

M.

N.

O.

P.

R.

S.

B 2

T.

U.

V.

W.

GENERAL RULES AND REGULATIONS.

1. All persons employed by the Company must devote themselves exclusively to the Company's service; they must reside at whatever places may be appointed, attend at such hours as may be required, pay prompt obedience to all persons placed in authority over them, and conform to all the Rules and Regulations of the Company.

Conditions of service.

2. The name and address of each servant employed in the working of the Railway must be registered at the Station to which he is attached, or at which he is paid, and the names and addresses of all persons connected with the Traffic Department (including Fog-signalmen) must be posted in the Station-master's Office, so that, if required in cases of emergency, the men may be readily found. Any change of address must be at once notified, in order that the record may be kept perfect.

Names and addresses of servants.

3. (*a*) No servant is allowed to absent himself from duty, to alter his appointed hours of attendance, or to exchange duty with any other servant, without the special permission of his superior officer. In case of illness, he must immediately report the circumstances to his superior officer.

Absence from, and exchange of, duty.

Illness.

(*b*) No Station-master must be absent without leave from the Superintendent, except from illness, in which case he must immediately inform the Superintendent, and take care that some competent person is entrusted with his duties,

Leave of absence of Station-master.

Illness.

Uniform—wearing and care of.

Property of the Company not to be appropriated to any servant's own use.

4. Every servant receiving uniform must, when on duty, appear in it clean and neat, with the number and badge perfect; and if any article provided by the Company be damaged by improper use, it must be made good by the servant using it. **No servant is allowed to appropriate to his own use any article, the property of the Company.**

Conduct of servants.

5. All servants must be prompt, civil, and obliging. They must afford every proper facility for the business to be performed, be careful to give correct information, and, when asked, give their names or numbers without hesitation.

Public safety of first importance.

6. The safety of the public must, under all circumstances, be the chief care of the servants of the Company.

Security for faithful service.

7. All persons holding situations of trust will be required to find security for their faithful services, the amount and conditions of which security will be stated upon appointment.

Insurance or Provident Societies.

8. The following Societies have been established or authorized by the Company, which the servants are required to join in accordance with the Regulations :—

(*a*) *Great Western Railway Superannuation Fund.*

(*b*) *Great Western Railway Guarantee Fund.*

(*c*) *Great Western Railway Provident Society.*

(*d*) *Great Western Railway Widows' and Orphans' Benevolent Fund.*

(*e*) *Great Western Railway Enginemen and Firemen's Mutual Assurance, Sick, and Superannuation Society.*

The following Society has also been established :—

The Great Western Railway Pension Society.

9. No servant, when on duty or in uniform, is allowed to enter a Station Refreshment-room, or any other Refreshment-room under the control of the Company, except by permission of the Station-master, or person in charge of the Station.

Refreshment room —entering without special permission forbidden.

10. No gratuity is allowed to be taken from passengers, or other persons, by any servant of the Company.

Gratuities not to be accepted.

11. No servant of the Company is allowed to trade, either directly or indirectly, for himself or others

Trading forbidden.

12. *The Company may at any time, without notice, dismiss or suspend from duty any servant of the Company for intoxication, disobedience of orders, negligence, or misconduct, or for being absent from duty without leave, and no wages shall be payable by the Company to any servant after his dismissal, or during the period of his suspension from duty, or during his absence from duty from any cause.*

Misconduct punishable.

The Company may impose the following fines in respect of the acts or omissions mentioned below, and deduct from the wages of persons in their employment the sums that are imposed as fines :—

Fines.

1. *For absence from duty without leave; coming late on duty; leaving duty before proper time or before being relieved; coming on duty without proper rest or otherwise unfit for duty; or permitting relief by men unauthorized or unfit for duty* ...	2*s.* 6*d.*

2. *For insubordination or non-observance of the lawful orders of a superior officer; for the use of abusive or offensive language whilst on duty; for the wilful misrepresentation or suppression of facts in a verbal or written report; or for failing to report irregularities or accidents ... ...*	2*s.* 6*d.*
3. *For incivility or want of proper courtesy or attention to Passengers or other members of the public ... ...*	
4. *For a repetition of any of the above offences*	5*s.*
5. *For negligence or misconduct by which delay is or may be caused to trains or traffic ...*	5*s.*
6. *For negligence or misconduct by which damage or injury is or may be caused to luggage, parcels, animals, goods or traffic; or to engines, vehicles, machines, signals, lamps, or other property of the Company ...*	
7. *For a repetition of such negligence or misconduct ... ...*	10*s.*
8. *For negligence or misconduct whereby danger or risk of danger is or may be caused to human life ... ...*	10*s.*
9. *For a repetition of such negligence or misconduct ... ...*	20*s.*

Leaving service—notice requisite.

13. No servant is allowed to leave the Company's service without giving the notice required by the terms of his engagement.

On leaving service, uniform and all property of the Company to be returned.

14. When a person leaves the service he must immediately deliver up his uniform and all other articles belonging to the Company. Any money that may be due for wages to any person leaving the service will not be paid until the clothing, book of rules, lamps, flags, tools, detonators, and all other articles the property of the Company, which may have been supplied to him, and of which he cannot give a satisfactory account, shall have been delivered up in accordance with the Company's Regulations. If not delivered up, or if any article be missing, or be damaged by improper use, the cost of such article, or of the

repair of such damage, shall be a debt due from the man to the Company, and may be deducted from any pay then due, or, if such pay be found insufficient to meet the claim, will become a debt recoverable at law.

15. The Company reserve the right to deduct from the pay of a servant, who is a tenant of the Company, any sums due for rent.

Rent.

16. All testimonials and letters of recommendation, except such as are addressed to the Company, or their officers, will, if required, be returned by the Company at the time the person whom they concern leaves the service.

Testimonials and letters of recommendation.

17 (*a*) Every Station-master, Inspector, Engine-driver, Fireman, Guard, Signalman, Policeman, Ganger, Foreman, Shunter, Yardman, and Gate-keeper; every Clerk, Porter and other servant connected with the working of the Railway; and also every man engaged on the Permanent-way or Works affecting the Running Lines, must be supplied with, and have with him when on duty, and produce when required, a copy of these Rules and Regulations.

Regulations Notices, and Working Time-table—to whom supplied.

(*b*) Except as shown below, every person above referred to must also be supplied with, and have with him when on duty, a copy of the current Working Time-table book, or section of the book, the Appendix thereto, where issued, and any Signalling, Permanent-way, or Special Train Notices; a copy of each must also be kept in the Station-master's Office.

Exceptions—(i.) *Where two or more men are employed at one Signal-box, it is not necessary to supply each man with a separate copy of the Working Time-table book or section of the book, as*

Exceptions.

the case may be, nor of the Appendix or other Notices, but one copy of each must be supplied for the use of all the men employed at the Signal-box.

(ii.) *At Stations where the Foremen, Porters, or other servants connected with the working of the traffic, use, or have ordinary access to, the Station-master's Office, it is not necessary to supply each man with a copy of the Working Time-table book, or section of the book, nor of the Appendix or other Notices, but a copy of each must be kept in the Station-master's Office, so as to be accessible for reference by those men. At Stations where the men do not use the Station-master's Office, a copy of each must be kept in a convenient place to which all engaged in the working of the traffic have ready access.*

(iii.) *It is not necessary to supply Firemen who have not been passed to act as Engine-drivers with the Working Time-tables or other Notices, but those supplied to an Engine-driver must be accessible to his Fireman.*

(iv.) *It is not necessary to supply the ordinary Labourers working under the supervision of Gangers or Foremen, with Working Time-tables or other Notices.*

Responsibility for supply of Notices.

(c) The Locomotive District Superintendents or Foremen, and Station-masters, are respectively responsible for a copy of every printed and written Notice of Signal and other alterations being supplied, as soon as possible after receipt, to each Engine-driver, Fireman who has been passed to act as Engine-driver, Guard and Porter-guard working over the Line affected by the Notice, and for his signature for the same being taken in the book provided for the purpose, which must be available for reference when required.

(*d*) Engine-drivers and Guards must obtain and carry with them when on duty all necessary Notices as to the signalling and general working of the Line.

Notices to be obtained.

(*e*) Where the trains of one Company run over the Lines of other Companies worked upon the Block Telegraph System, it is not necessary to supply the servants of the running Company with the Working Time-table, Appendix thereto, and Special Train Notices of the Company owning the Line, it being considered sufficient that such servants be supplied with any special instructions affecting the working of that portion of the Line over which the trains pass.

Where trains run over other Companies' Lines.

18. If any servant lose his copy of the Rules and Regulations, Time-table, Appendix, or other document of which the Regulations require that he should be in possession, he must immediately obtain another copy from his superior officer.

Lost copies of Regulations, &c., to be replaced.

19. Every servant must assist in carrying out the Rules and Regulations, and immediately report to his superior officer any infringement thereof, or any occurrence which may come under his notice affecting the safe and proper working of the traffic.

Servants to assist in carrying out Regulations

20. (*a*) No person must be allowed to travel on the Railway, unless provided with a proper ticket or free pass; and no officer or servant of the Company must be allowed, unless in the execution of his duty, to ride on the engine, or in the break-van, or in any vehicle in which luggage or parcels are conveyed, without written or printed permission from a properly authorised officer of the Company.

Travelling without pass or ticket forbidden.

Riding on engine, or in break-van without special authority forbidden.

(*b*) Except persons provided with proper tickets travelling in charge of Live Stock, no person, other than a servant of the Company in the execution of his duty, must be allowed to travel

Persons not to travel by Goods train without special authority.

by a goods train, either with a pass or ticket, without special authority from a properly authorised officer.

Luggage left by passengers not to be taken charge of by servants.

21. The Company's servants must not take charge of luggage or other articles left at the Station for the convenience of passengers. All such luggage or articles must be deposited in the Cloak Room in the regular manner.

Unclaimed luggage, &c.

22. All unclaimed or lost luggage, money, or other property found in the carriages, at the Stations, or upon the Line, must be immediately delivered to the person in charge of the Station at, or nearest to, the place where the article has been found, and be dealt with by him in accordance with the Company's instructions upon the subject.

Getting between vehicles to couple or uncouple them.

23. (*a*) All servants must exercise proper care in getting between vehicles for the purpose of coupling or uncoupling them, and Shunting Poles or Sticks must be used when practicable.

Porters meeting trains at Stations.

(*b*) When a train is entering a Station, Porters must stand a few yards apart, a short distance from the edge of the platform, until the train has stopped, when they must attend to the compartments which are opposite to them, irrespective of class.

Not to jump on to steps or footboards of trains.

(*c*) No servant must jump on to the steps or footboards, or run alongside, of trains entering Stations.

Servants not to expose themselves to danger.

24. (*a*) The servants of the Company, more especially those engaged in the working of trains and in shunting and other similiar operations, must not expose themselves to danger; and all are requested to prevent, as far as they possibly can, such exposure on the part of their fellow-servants, and to spare no opportunity of warning those who neglect to take proper care.

(*b*) Reckless exposure of himself or others to danger, on the part of any servant of the Company, will be treated as an offence against the Company's Regulations, and punished accordingly.

25. (*a*) No person, other than a servant of the Company in the execution of his duty, must be allowed to be, or walk, upon the Railway, unless provided with written or printed permission to do so, signed by a properly authorised officer of the Company.

Trespassing

(*b*) Unless instructions are issued to the contrary, any person trespassing must be requested to leave the Company's premises, and, on complying, must be warned not to go or pass thereon again. If such person refuse to quit, he must be requested to give his name and address, which must be handed to the nearest Station-master or other superior officer with a report of the circumstances. In the event of the offender refusing his name and address, he must be detained and given in charge of the Police.

NOTE.—*See addition to this Rule in the Appendix to the Rule Book.*

26. The Company's servants must not walk upon the Line, except when it is necessary for them to do so in the execution of their duty.

Company's servants trespassing.

27. (*a*) Except where otherwise provided, when the word "Train" is used it must be understood to include "Light-engine," *i.e.*, engine without a train.

"Train" includes "Light-engine."

(*b*) When the words "Goods train" are used they must be understood to include all trains except those composed of coaching stock.

Definition of Goods trains.

(*c*) Mixed trains conveying Passengers and Goods must be dealt with as Passenger trains.

Mixed trains.

SIGNALS.

FIXED SIGNALS.

Fixed Signals.

28. Fixed Signals consist of Distant, Home, Starting, Advanced Starting, Siding, Calling-on, and Shunting Signals.

NOTE.—*See addition to this Rule in the Appendix to the Rule Book.*

Normal position of Fixed Signals.

29. The normal position of Fixed Signals is Danger, except where otherwise provided in these Rules, or by the special authority of the General Manager or Superintendent of the Line.

RED is a signal of "**DANGER,**"
GREEN ,, "**ALL RIGHT.**"

Semaphore Signals adopted on majority of Lines.

30. On the majority of Lines, Semaphore Signals are adopted, but other forms of Signals are used by some Companies.

Semaphore Arms and Lamps.

31. The Semaphore Signals are constructed with Arms for Day Signals, and Lamps for Night.

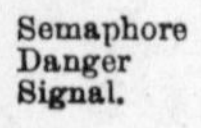

Semaphore Danger Signal.

32. The Semaphore Danger Signal is shown, in the day time, by the Arm being in the horizontal position, thus:—

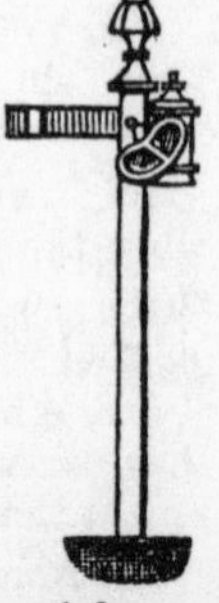

and by the exhibition of a Red Light by night.

NOTE.—*On some Companies' Lines, a Purple or White Light is used as the Danger Signal for controlling Sidings and Bay Lines.*

For Great Western practice see Appendix to Rule Book.

33. The Semaphore All Right Signal is shown, in the daytime, by the Arm being lowered, thus :—

Semaphore All Right Signal.

and by the exhibition of a Green Light by night.

NOTE.—*On some Companies' Lines the Arm is lowered parallel with the post, thus :—*

DISTANT SIGNALS.

Distant Signals.

34. (*a*) Distant Signals are fixed at some distance from the point at which the Home Signal is placed, and where Semaphores are used as Distant Signals the Arms are notched or swallow-tailed, thus:—

Distant Signal on Home, Starting, or Advanced Starting Signal post.

(*b*) Where it is found necessary to place the Distant Signal Arm worked from a Signal-box in advance on the post of the Home, Starting, or Advanced Starting Signal applicable to the same Line, of the Box in the rear, the Distant Signal will be the lower, and the Home, Starting, or Advanced Starting Signal the upper, Arm of that post.

Use of Distant Signal.

35. Distant Signals must be placed at Danger immediately they are passed by a train, and also whenever any obstruction or danger exists upon the Line they are intended to protect.

Observance of Distant Signal.

36. When an Engine-driver finds a Distant Signal at Danger he must reduce speed and proceed cautiously towards the Home Signal, being prepared to stop if necessary.

Distant Signal fixed near to another Box.

37. Where the Distant Signal worked from one Box is fixed near to another Box, the Signalman on duty at the Box near to which the Signal is fixed will be held responsible for seeing that the Signal is in working order, and that the light of such Signal is burning properly when necessary. This will not, however, relieve the Signalman from whose Box the Distant Signal is worked from satisfying himself that the Signal is working correctly.

HOME SIGNALS.

38. Home Signals are fixed at Stations, Junctions, Sidings, and Signal-boxes, and, as a rule, are so placed as to indicate by their positions the Lines to which they apply; when more Arms than one are fixed on the same side of a post they apply generally as follow, viz. :— Home Signals.

The first or top Arm, to the Line on the left;

The second Arm, to the Line next in order from the left;

and so on.

39. (*a.*) No train must pass a Home Signal at Danger, or foul the Crossings or Points to which it applies, except as prescribed in Rules 73 and 232, or where a Calling-on Arm is in use. Home Signal not to be passed at Danger, except where otherwise provided.

(*b*) When a train has been stopped, or brought nearly to a stand, at a Home Signal, and it is necessary to bring it within the Home Signal before the Section ahead is clear, the Signalman must, where a Starting Signal is provided, and that Signal is at Danger, lower the Home Signal for the train to draw ahead. Trains required to be brought within such Signals.

40. (*a*) When the Starting Signal is at Danger the Home Signal must not be lowered for an approaching train until the train is close to the Home Signal, and has been brought quite, or nearly, to a stand at it. In foggy weather or during falling snow the Engine-driver must, when practicable, be verbally informed that he is only to draw forward towards the Starting Signal. Home Signal not to be lowered for train which has to stop at Starting Signal until train is close to Home Signal.

Driver to go slowly forward when Home Signal is lowered, but not to pass out of sight of Signalman.

(*b*) The Engine-driver of any train which has been thus stopped, or brought nearly to a stand, at a Home Signal, must, after that Signal has been lowered, go slowly forward towards the Starting Signal, but must only proceed as far as is necessary to leave the last vehicle well clear of the Points and Crossings and within sight of the Signalman. The Starting Signal must not be passed until it is lowered, except as provided in Rule 44.

Starting Signal not to be passed until lowered.

Driver to stop at Signal-box if necessary.

(*c*) If the Signal-box is between the Home and Starting Signals the Engine-driver must be prepared to stop at the Box if necessary.

When trains are allowed to go forward under "Section Clear but Station or Junction Blocked" signal.

(*d*) When trains are allowed to go forward under the "Section Clear but Station or Junction Blocked" Signal (Block Telegraph Rule 5), the Signalman must, if the train has not already passed the Home Signal towards the Starting or Advanced Starting Signal, bring the train to a stand at the Home Signal, and verbally instruct the Engine-driver that the Section is clear to the next Home Signal, but that the Station or Junction ahead is Blocked. A Green Flag by day and a Green Light by night, held steadily in the hand, must at the same time be exhibited to the Engine-driver, and the necessary Fixed Signals lowered to give permission for the train to proceed.

Where Home Signal is at a distance from Signal-box.

(*e*) Where the Home Signal is at such a distance from the Signal-box that it is not possible for the Signalman to communicate verbally with the Driver when the engine is standing at the Home Signal, and there is no Calling-on Arm, the Signalman must, after bringing the train to a stand at the Home Signal, lower it to allow the Engine-driver to draw to his Box, and must stop the train at the Box by exhibiting a Red Flag by day and a Red Light by night. The Engine-driver must then be verbally instructed that the Section is clear to the next Home Signal, but that the Station or Junction ahead is blocked; after which a Green Flag by day and a Green Light by night, held steadily in the hand, must be exhibited to the Engine-driver, and the necessary Fixed Signals lowered to give permission for the train to proceed.

When train is assisted by engine in rear.

(*f*) If the train is assisted by an engine in the rear, a Green Flag by day and a Green Light by night, held steadily in the hand, must also be exhibited to the Driver of the engine in the rear of the train.

Train stopped at Home Signal where no Starting Signal.

41. (*a*) At places where Starting Signals are not provided, when a train has been stopped at the Home Signal, and it is necessary to draw it within such Signal before the Line ahead is clear, the Signalman must lower the Home Signal after verbally instructing the Engine-driver to bring his train under the protection of the Home Signal.

Train required to be brought within such Home Signal.

(*b*) Where the Home Signal is at such a distance from the Signal-box that it is not possible for the Signalman to communicate verbally with the Driver when the engine is standing at the Home Signal, and there is no Calling-on Arm, the Signalman must, after bringing the train to a stand at the Home Signal, lower it to allow the Engine-driver to draw to his Box, and must stop the train at the Box by exhibiting a Red Flag by day and a Red Light by night, and then, by verbal instructions, give the Engine-driver clearly to understand the state of the Line ahead.

Engine-drivers to clearly understand verbal communication.

(*c*) Engine-drivers must not go forward until they clearly understand the verbal communication which the Signalman has made to them as to the state of the Line ahead, and then only with their engines under the needful control to ensure safety.

(*d*) When the Line is clear the Signal for the train to proceed must be given by the Signalman showing the Engine-driver a Green Light by night and a Green Flag by day, held steadily in the hand.

Use of Home Signal.

42. Whenever the Distant Signal is at Danger the Danger Signal must also be exhibited at the Home Signal, except when a train has passed the Distant Signal at Danger, in which case the Home Signal only must be lowered to allow the train to pass.

CALLING-ON SIGNALS.

Calling-on Arms.

43. (*a*) Where short Arms are fixed upon the Home Signal posts as Calling-on Signals they are placed below the Home Signal. When a Calling-on Arm is lowered the Engine-driver must draw forward past the post of the Signal on which the Calling-on Arm is fixed, as far as the Line is clear. If, after lowering the Calling-on Arm, the Signalman wishes to communicate with the Engine-driver, and the Signal-box is ahead of the Calling-on Arm, he must show a Hand Danger Signal from the Box to stop him. The lowering of the Calling-on Arm is not an authority for a Starting Signal to be passed at Danger.

(*b*) Unless instructions are issued to the contrary, the Calling-on Arm must not be lowered until the train has been brought to a stand at the Home Signal.

STARTING AND ADVANCED STARTING SIGNALS.

Starting and Advanced Starting Signals not to be passed at Danger.

44. Starting Signals (where Advanced Starting Signals are not provided), and Advanced Starting Signals control the entrance of trains into the Section ahead, and must not be passed when at Danger, except as follow:—

Exceptions.

(*a*) *Where there are Shunting Arms. See Rule 46.*

(*b*) *When Signal is defective. See Rule 73.*

(*c*) *Single Line Working during Obstruction. See Rule 232.*

(*d*) *Where the Points of Sidings or Crossover-roads are so near to a Starting or Advanced Starting Signal as to render it necessary for the Signal to be passed for shunting purposes, and a Shunting Arm is not provided, Engine-drivers may, for the purpose of performing shunting operations, pass the Starting or Advanced Starting Signal when at Danger upon being directed to do so by the Signalman, either verbally or by a Green Hand Signal, which must be held steadily in the hand, but they must not proceed on their journey until the Starting or Advanced Starting Signal has been lowered.*

Line clear between Starting and Advanced Starting Signals.

45. (*a*) Where Advanced Starting Signals are provided the Starting Signal must not be passed at Danger, but when the Line is clear between the Starting and Advanced Starting Signals, and the Advanced Starting Signal is at Danger, the Signalman must, when necessary, after a train has been brought to a stand, lower the Starting Signal to allow such train to proceed towards the Advanced Starting Signal.

When Starting Signal to be put to Danger.

(*b*) When a train has gone forward into the Section in advance, the Starting or Advanced Starting Signal which controls the entrance of trains into such Section must be put to, and kept at, Danger, until it is again necessary to lower it for a following train to pass, in accordance with the prescribed Regulations. So long as the Starting Signal is at Danger, the Home and Distant Signals must also be kept at Danger until a following train is close to the Home Signal, and has been brought quite, or nearly, to a stand at it, when that Signal may be lowered so as to admit of the train stopping at the platform or at the Starting Signal.

Home and Distant Signals to be kept at Danger when Starting Signal at Danger.

When train brought to a stand at Starting or Advanced Starting Signals.

(*c*) Except where instructions are issued to the contrary, when a train has passed the Signal-box and is brought to a stand at the Starting or Advanced Starting Signal, the Engine-driver must understand that the lowering of the Starting or Advanced Starting Signal is an indication that the Line is only clear to the Home Signal at the Signal-box in advance, and that he must regulate the speed of his train in the same way as if he had been verbally instructed to proceed under the "Section Clear but Station or Junction Blocked" signal.

(*d*) In foggy weather or during falling snow trains waiting "Line Clear" must, as far as practicable, be kept within the sight of the Signalman, and, unless special instructions are issued to the contrary, no train must be drawn past the Starting Signal towards the Advanced Starting Signal, except for Station duties or Shunting purposes.

Use of Advanced Starting Signal in foggy weather or during falling snow.

SHUNTING SIGNALS.

46. Where these Signals are fixed as lower Arms upon the Starting or Advanced Starting Signal posts, the lowering of the Shunting Arm authorises an Engine-driver to pass, for shunting purposes only, the Starting or Advanced Starting Signal when at Danger, but no train must go forward on its journey until the Starting or Advanced Starting Signal is lowered.

Shunting Signals.

DISC OR DWARF SIGNALS.

47. (*a*) Where these Signals are used to regulate the passage of trains between Sidings and Running Lines, or between one Running Line and another, or Shunting operations in Sidings, the Danger Signal is shown, in the daytime by a Red Disc, or Dwarf Signal with a Short Arm, and at night by a Red Light.

Disc or Dwarf Signals.

(*b*) The All Right Signal is shown, in the daytime, by the Disc being turned off, or the Arm being lowered, and at night by a Green Light.

Note.—*On some Companies' Lines a Purple or small White Light is used as the Danger*

Signal for Ground Discs controlling Sidings, Crossover-roads, and Bay Lines, and on other Companies' Lines no light is shown to indicate the Danger position.

For Great Western practice see Appendix to Rule Book.

SIDING SIGNALS.

Siding Signals.

48. (*a*) When the exit from Sidings is controlled by Disc or Semaphore Signals no attempt must be made to take a train from such Sidings until the Signal is turned off or lowered, nor must an Engine-driver, whilst waiting for such Signal to be turned off or lowered, allow his engine to stand foul of any other Line.

(*b*) When a Signal applies to more than one Siding, and more than one Engine is in the Sidings at the same time, no Engine-driver must move towards the Signal until he has been instructed to do so by the Foreman Shunter or other person in charge.

BACK LIGHTS OF FIXED SIGNALS.

Back Lights of Fixed Signals.

49. The Back Lights of Fixed Signals show a White Light to the Signalman when at Danger, and a Purple Light or no Light when at All Right.

HAND SIGNALS.

Hand Signals.

50. (*a*) These Signals will be made with Flags by day, and with Lamps by night and in foggy weather or during falling snow. A Red Light or a Red Flag is a Signal of Danger—Stop; in the absence of a Red Light, any light waved violently denotes Danger.

(*b*) The purposes for which a White or a Green Hand Signal is used are as follow :—

1.—Move forward, in shunting—Rule 52.	White Light waved slowly up and down.
2.—Move back, in shunting—Rule 52.	White Light waved slowly from side to side across body.
3.—Move forward slowly, in shunting—Rule 52.	Green Light waved slowly up and down.
4.—Move back slowly, in shunting—Rule 52.	Green Light waved slowly from side to side across body.
5.—Guard's signal to Engine-driver to start, and to indicate that Guard or Shunter has rejoined train.—Rules 55 and 171.	By day, Green Flag (where used). By night, Green Light, held steadily above the head.
6.—To indicate by night to Engine-driver of Goods train after starting that his train is complete.—Rule 171.	Green Light waved slowly from side to side by Guard from his van.
7.—To indicate to Engine-driver that train is divided.—Rule 220.	Green Light or Flag waved slowly from side to side by Signalman.
8.—To give an All Right Signal to Engine-driver where there is no Starting Signal.—Rule 41.	Green Light or Flag held steadily in the hand by Signalman.
9.—To authorise Engine-driver to pass Starting Signal at Danger, for shunting purposes.—Rule 44.	Green Light or Flag held steadily in the hand by Signalman.
10.—To indicate to Engine-driver in foggy weather or during falling snow that the Signal is at All Right.—Rules 81 and 144	Green Light or Flag held steadily in the hand by Fog-signalman.

11.—To reduce speed for Permanent-way operations. —Rules 76, 155, 244, and 253.	Green Light or Flag waved slowly from side to side by Platelayer.
12.—To give an All-right Signal to Engine-driver when Fixed Signal is disconnected or out of order.—Rule 73.	Green Light or Flag held steadily by Hand-signalman at the Signal.
13.—To indicate to Engine-driver that Section is clear, but Station or Junction is blocked.—Rule 40.	Green Light or Flag held steadily by Signalman after bringing train to a stand and giving verbal warning.
14.—To indicate to Engine-driver of Goods train, timed to stop at a Station, that there is nothing to pick up, and that if he has nothing to put off he may run through.—Rule 173.	Green Light or Flag waved slowly up and down.
15.—To indicate that Catch Points are in right position for train to pass in facing direction.—Rule 236.	Green Light or Flag held steadily in the hand by man at Points.
16.—To caution Engine-driver entering Terminal Station, or Station worked under special instructions, if Line is not clear.—Rule 87.	Green Light or Flag held steadily in the hand by Signalman after bringing train to a stand and giving verbal warning.
17—To caution Engine-driver of following train on Time Interval system. —Time Interval Regulation 3. (Appendix to Rule Book.)	Green Light or Flag held steadily in the hand by Signalman after bringing train to a stand and giving verbal warning.
18.—To indicate to Engine-driver that slip portion is detached.—Slip Carriage Regulation 7. (Appendix to Rule Book.)	Green Light or Flag waved slowly up and down by Slip Guard.

51. *In the absence of Flags—*

(*a*) Both arms raised above the head denotes Danger, thus :—

Danger Signal.

(*b*) One arm raised above the head denotes Caution, thus :—

Caution Signal.

(*c*) One arm held in a horizontal position denotes All Right, thus :—

All Right Signal.

Shunting Signals by night.

52. (*a*) In shunting operations by night, or when necessary in foggy weather or during falling snow, a White Light waved slowly up and down means "Move forward," *i.e.*, go away from the person giving the signal; a White Light waved slowly from side to side across the body means "Move back," *i.e.*, come towards the person giving the signal.

(*b*) A Green Light used instead of a White Light, as above, means "Move forward slowly," or "Move back slowly."

Hand Signals to be held in hand.

53. Hand Lamps and Flags, when used as Signals, except where they are employed for the purpose of marking the actual point of obstruction, must always be held in the hand, and not placed upon, or stuck into, the ground, or fixed elsewhere.

SIGNALLING IN CONNECTION WITH TRAINS SHUNTING OR RUNNING IN WRONG DIRECTION.

Distant, Home, Starting, & Advanced Starting Signals apply only to trains running in proper direction. Mode of signalling during shunting, and of signalling trains running in wrong direction.

54. Distant, Home, Starting, and Advanced Starting Signals apply only to trains travelling in the proper Direction on the Running Lines, and must not be used for any other purpose, except as provided in Rule 232. Trains moving in the wrong direction on any Running Line must be signalled by Hand Lamp or Flag. Trains shunting from one Running Line to another, or shunting into, or out of, Sidings connected with Running Lines, must, unless Fixed Signals are provided for the purpose of signalling such operations, be signalled either verbally, or by Hand Lamp or Flag, as occasion may require; it being necessary, in such cases, that the Fixed Signals should be kept at Danger for the protection of the trains so employed.

DETENTION AT HOME OR STARTING SIGNALS.

Driver to whistle, and Signalman to be reminded by Guard, Shunter, or Fireman of position of train.

55. (*a*) In case of detention at a Home, Starting, or Advanced Starting Signal, the Enginedriver must immediately sound his whistle, and, if still detained, the Guard, Shunter, or Fireman must (except where instructions are given to the contrary, or where the Lock and Block system of Train signalling is in operation) go into the Signal-box and remind the Signalman of the position of the train, and remain there until the Signalman can give permission for it to go forward. In foggy weather or during falling snow the Guard, Shunter, or Fireman must, immediately upon the train coming to a stand, proceed to the Signal-box.

Guard, Shunter, or Fireman to go to Signal-box.

(*b*) When a train or vehicles have passed a Home Signal, and are waiting to be crossed to another Line, or to be let into a Siding, or have been shunted on to the opposite running Line, or placed on either a Main or Branch Line at a Junction, or when a train or vehicles have been shunted from a Siding on to a Running Line, and are waiting to be crossed to another Line, the Guard, Shunter, or Fireman must, when the train or vehicles come to a stand, proceed immediately to the Signal-box, and remind the Signalman of the position of the train or vehicles, and remain in the Box until the Signalman can give permission for them to proceed, or to be shunted clear of the Running Lines.

(c) The duty of going to the Signalman must be performed as under :—

(i.) In the case of a light-engine, or of a Passenger train with only one Guard, by the Fireman; the Guard in the latter case remaining in charge of the train.

(ii.) In the case of a Goods train with only one Guard—

When stopped at a Home Signal, by the Fireman.

When stopped at a Starting or Advanced Starting Signal, by the Guard.

When waiting to be crossed on to another Line or to be let into a Siding, by the Guard.

When crossed to the opposite Line, by the Fireman.

When drawn ahead on to a Main or Branch Line at a Junction, by the Guard.

When backed on to a Main or Branch Line at a Junction, by the Fireman.

(iii.) In the case of a train with two or more Guards, by the Guard whose van is nearest to the Signal-box; if there is only one van on the train, by the Under-guard.

(iv.) In the case of there being a Guard as well as a Shunter with the train or vehicles, then the Guard must go to the Signal-box.

(v.) In the case of a **train or vehicles in** charge only of a Shunter, the Shunter must go to the Signal-box.

(*d*) The Guard in charge of the train must satisfy himself that the man whose duty it is to do so has gone to the Signal-box; and the Guard or Shunter, as the case may be, will be held responsible for seeing that the train or vehicles are properly secured.

(*e*) When a train or vehicles have been shunted from one Running Line to another, the Guard or Shunter, as the case may be, must, before going to the Signal-box, satisfy himself that the Line from which the train or vehicles have been shunted is clear.

Time to be allowed for man to rejoin his van or engine before Signal is lowered.

(*f*) Sufficient time must be allowed for the Guard, Shunter, or Fireman to rejoin the train before the Signal is lowered, and the Engine-driver must not, when the Signal is lowered, go forward until he has received a Hand Signal from the Guard or Shunter to intimate that he has rejoined the train. By day the Hand Signal will be the All Right Signal in accordance with Rule 51, or (where used) by the exhibition of a Green Flag, and by night a Green Light held steadily above the head.

Man to satisfy himself Signalman is aware of obstruction.

(*g*) The man who goes to the Signal-box as a reminder to the Signalman, must satisfy himself by personal inquiry that the Signalman is aware of the obstruction, and has protected the train.

Where mechanical or other appliances are used as reminder to Signalman.

(*h*) Where mechanical or other appliances are provided to serve as a reminder to the Signalman that certain Signals must not be lowered or turned off, he must make prompt use of such appliances; and the Guard, Shunter, or Fireman, who has gone into the Signal-box in accordance with clauses (*a*) and (*b*) must, after satisfying himself that this has been done, return to his train. In addition, where the Company's Regulations require it, the Signalman must "Block Back" to the Signal-box or Boxes affected by the obstruction before allowing the Line to be obstructed.

WORKING OF POINTS AND SIGNALS.

Points, Signals, Interlocking and other apparatus to be examined, and reported when defective.

56. The Signalman on duty must see that the Points, Signals, Interlocking, Electric, and other apparatus are kept in perfect working order; and he must immediately report to the Station-master under whose supervision he acts, and to the Inspector of Permanent-way or other person in charge of repairs, any case in which the Points, Signals, or Interlocking arrangements are out of repair, or not properly cleaned and oiled; and the Station-master must, where necessary, telegraph the circumstances to the proper authorities. The Signalman is responsible for exhibiting outside his Signal-box the Boards prescribed to indicate the state of the Electric and other Apparatus connected with his Signal-box, and he must immediately report any defect to the Station-master.

Damage to Points, Rails, or Crossings to be reported.

57. When, from the passage of a train or other cause, any Point, Crossing, or Check Rail is damaged or strained, or the Rails themselves are split or strained, the circumstances must immediately be reported to the Station-master and Inspector of Permanent-way, Foreman

Platelayer, or Ganger, and all trains must be stopped, or allowed to pass over slowly, as may be necessary, until the damage is repaired.

58. The Signalman must frequently examine and try his Fixed Signals to see that they work well, are kept clean, and show properly. Care must be used in putting a Signal to Danger; it is not sufficient merely to move the lever, but the Signalman must, at the same time, watch the Signal so as to ascertain that it obeys the lever and goes fully to Danger. Where a Fixed Signal is out of the Signalman's sight, and its working is indicated by a Repeater in the Signal-box, he must satisfy himself by observation of the Repeater that the Fixed Signal is working properly. He must take care that the Signal wires are kept properly adjusted by means of the regulating screws or links, so as to compensate for the expansion and contraction caused by variations of temperature.

Signals to be frequently examined.

Care in putting Signal to Danger.

Wires to be regulated.

59. Should any impediment or obstruction exist upon the Line within the sight or knowledge of the Signalman, he must place or keep the necessary Fixed Signals at Danger, and prevent any train passing his Box in that direction, until such impediment or obstruction has been removed and the Line made perfectly clear and safe.

Signals to be exhibited in case of obstruction.

60. (*a*) When a train is approaching Facing Points the Signalman must see that the lever which governs them is close home to the frame, and that the catch is firmly down in the notch, and remains so until the whole of the train has passed. He must also, from observation, when practicable, assure himself that the Points have obeyed the lever and are in the proper position.

Facing Points.

(*b*) Facing Points must be frequently tested by the Signalman so that he may satisfy himself they work well, and that no part is damaged.

(*c*) Facing Points not worked from a Locking-frame must be securely fastened or held for the passage of each train.

Signal to be replaced at Danger after passage of train.

61. When a Signal other than a Distant Signal has been lowered for the passing of a train, it must not (except in case of accident or obstruction, or as provided for in Rule 64) be again placed at Danger until the last vehicle of the train has passed it, or the train has been brought to a stand; nor, in the case of a Junction, until the last vehicle of the train has passed it, and is clear of the Junction Points.

Shunting carriages and other vehicles.

62. (*a*) Signalmen must exercise great care in shunting carriages and other vehicles. They must not move the Points until they have obtained a signal from the Guard or Shunter, or from the Engine-driver or Fireman in the case of a light engine, that the last vehicle or the light engine, as the case may be, is clear of the Points.

(*b*) After shunting operations of any description the Signalman must see, or have intimation from the Guard (or if a Shunter has been employed, then from him), that the carriages or other vehicles have been left secure in the Sidings, and that the Running Lines are clear before lowering the Signals to allow any train to pass. In the case of a light-engine, the Fireman will be held responsible for so advising the Signalman.

(*c*) When it is necessary to shunt vehicles on any Running Line, the Guard or Shunter must satisfy himself that, in the shunting operations, none of the vehicles have become detached, and are left upon any Running Line.

Catch Points.

63. Where Catch Points are worked from Signal-boxes Signalmen must, in order to prevent any vehicle running back on the Line in which the Catch Points are provided, keep the Points open for the runaway end, except when required to be closed for trains to pass over them on the Running Line. Should it be necessary to move a train in the wrong direction on the Line provided with Catch Points (whether worked from a Signal-box or not), care must be taken that the Points are right for the direction in which the train is moving.

When two trains approach a Junction at same time or nearly same time.

64. (*a*) If, when two or more trains approach a Junction at the same time or at nearly the same time, the Signalman should have lowered or taken off the Signals for a train which should have been kept back for the passage of another, he must not attempt to alter the order of the trains by reversing the Signals, but must place them all at Danger, and so keep them until all the trains have been brought to a stand, when precedence can be given to the proper train.

Reversing of Signals.

(*b*) When, after a Signal has been taken off for a train to leave a Station or Siding, it is necessary for the Signal to be replaced to Danger before the train starts, the Signalman must, when practicable, before he allows any obstruction of the line to which the Signal applies, satisfy himself that the Engine-driver is aware of the

Signal having been reversed. This, however, will not relieve the Engine-driver of the responsibility of satisfying himself, by personal observation, before starting, that the proper Signal is off for him to proceed.

Signals, &c., not to be interfered with by unauthorised persons.

65. (*a*) No unauthorised person must be allowed to interfere with the working of the Signals or Points, or the Electrical Instruments or Bells.

Points not to be moved without Signalman's permission.

(*b*) No person must move any Points which lead to a Running Line, or from one Running Line to another, without the permission of the Signalman in charge.

Signal-box to be kept private.

66. (*a*) Each Signalman must keep his Signal-box strictly private, and not allow any other persons than the authorised officers and servants of the Company to enter it.

Signal-box to be kept clean.

(*b*) Signal-boxes, and the Instruments and other appliances therein, must be kept in proper order and perfectly clean.

Lighting Signal Lamps.

67. (*a*) The Signal Lamps must be lighted as soon as it commences to be dusk, and in foggy weather or during falling snow.

Extinguishing Signal Lamps.

(*b*) At places which are open all night the Signal Lamps must not, unless instructions are issued to the contrary, be extinguished until broad daylight.

Places closed during night.

(*c*) At places which are closed during the night the Signal Lamps must, unless instructions are issued to the contrary, be extinguished after the Signal-box has been closed, and, if the Box has to be opened in the morning before daylight, they must be re-lighted in sufficient time for the passage of the first train.

Danger Signal to be shown when Signalman leaves his Box temporarily

68. Unless instructions are issued to the contrary, when it is necessary for a Signalman to leave his Signal-box for the purpose of re-lighting or re-trimming any of his Signal Lamps, he must not do so unless all his Signals are at Danger.

Signalman leaving duty to give information to man by whom he is relieved.

69. Every Signalman, before taking charge of a Signal-box, must satisfy himself that all the Electrical Instruments, Signals, Points, &c., are in good working order, and, when relieving another Signalman, must ascertain from him whether there is any special circumstance requiring attention; whether the trains which are due to pass have done so, and if not, what are the exceptions; and what trains, if any, are in the section on either side of his Signal-box, or are signalled. He must also ascertain whether there is any other matter, the knowledge of which is necessary to enable him to properly discharge his duty. The Signalman relieved must give full information on these points before leaving duty, so that the duties of the Box may be conducted in an efficient manner, and any inconvenience arising from the change of men avoided. Each Signalman must enter in the Train Register Book the time of his arrival on duty and the time of his leaving, and place his signature thereto. Signalmen must change duty only at the appointed hours.

FIXING, REMOVING, OR REPAIRING SIGNALS OR APPARATUS FOR WORKING POINTS AND SIGNALS.

Erection or removal of Signals, or other work in connection with Points or Signals.

70. Before the erection or removal of Signals, or the prosecution of other work in connection with Points or Signals which may interfere with the safe working of the Line, the Foreman Signal-fitter who has charge of the work must, unless the work has been previously arranged for between the Signalling and the Traffic Departments, and the necessary notice issued by the General Manager or the Superintendent of the Line, communicate with the District Superintendent, Traffic Inspector, or Station-master, as the case may be, who will make any special arrangements that may be necessary in connection with the working of the traffic during the time such alterations or repairs are being effected. Where there is no Station-master or Signalman, and no special arrangements have been made with the Traffic Department, Signal-fitters must provide for the safety of the Line in accordance with Rule 250.

Disarrangement of Interlocking or disconnection of Signals, Points, &c.

71. (*a*) When the work involves the disarrangement of the Interlocking apparatus, or the disconnection of Signals, Points, Facing Point Bars or Locks, Fouling Bars, Detectors, Bridge Bolts, Turntable Bolts, or Level Crossing Gates, the Signal-fitter must, before the work is commenced, give to the Signalman an exact description of the nature of the work, and the Signalman must enter in the Train Register or Book provided for the purpose the words "Locking disarranged," with the numbers of the levers which will be interfered with; both he and the Signal-fitter must sign their names, and the time must be recorded.

(*b*) When the work involves the disarrangement of the Interlocking, or when it is necessary to disconnect a Facing Point, Facing Point Bar or Lock, Bridge Bolt, or Turntable Bolt, the Signal-fitter must, before the work is commenced, disconnect and fix at Danger the Distant Signals applicable to the Lines affected.

Hand-signalman.

(*c*) A Hand-signalman to work under the instructions of the Signalman must be provided, and act in accordance with Rule 73.

(*d*) Before interfering with the Locking connections, the Signal-fitter must satisfy himself that the Hand-signalman is at his post.

Signalman to communicate with Hand-signalman.

(*e*) During the time the Points are disconnected the Signalman must, on each occasion when he requires to pass a train over the Points, communicate with the Hand-signalman, and receive his assurance that all Points concerned are in their proper position and secured.

Men at Points to assist Hand-signalman.

(*f*) In cases where, owing to a number of Points being disconnected from the Signal-box, it may be necessary to place a man at each pair of Points, or to attend to a number of Points, these men must receive their instructions from the Signalman as to the duties they have to perform. When a train is required to be sent over Points which are being attended to by the men assisting the Hand-signalman, the Hand-signalman must so inform such men, and take care that they properly secure the Points for the Line on which the train is to pass, and the Points must not again be altered in position until the Hand-signalman has advised them that the operation is completed. When this has been done, the men will be at liberty to move the Points as may be required to suit the convenience of the Signal-fitters working at them, it being understood that no train will be sent over them, without previous intimation being given in each case by the Hand-signalman.

Repairs to Level Crossing Gates.

(*g*) When carrying out repairs to Level Crossing Gates involving the disconnection of the Interlocking, the Signal-fitter must disconnect and fix at Danger the Distant Signals, and a Hand-signalman must be provided to attend to the working of the Gates and the protection of the Crossing.

When work completed.

(*h*) When the work is completed, the Signalman, after receiving an assurance from the Signal-fitter that all is right, must test the Locking, and, if found to be all right, then enter in the Train Register or Book provided for the purpose the words "Locking restored," and both he and the Signal-fitter must sign their names under the words, a note of the time being also inserted.

When Fixed Signal disconnected and Interlocking is right.

(*i*) When any Fixed Signal is out of order or is disconnected for repair or otherwise, or when any Points are disconnected and the Interlocking of the Point and Signal Levers is all right, the Signalman must, to enable him to obtain the security of the Interlocking, use the lever applicable to such Signal or Points, as if the Signal or Points were in work, and the Signal and Counter-balance weight must, when necessary be disconnected by the Signal-fitter from the lever to admit of this being done.

(*j*) When the Interlocking of any Signal or Point is being repaired, altered or cleaned by the Signal-fitter, the Signal-fitter must not (except for testing purposes, and then only with the permission of the Signalman) move any lever but must ask the Signalman to move it for him; nor must the Signalman move any lever connected with any Point or Signal at which the Signal-fitter is at work without first obtaining his permission.

Signal-fitter not to move levers without Signalman's permission.

72. (*a*) No new Signal must be brought into use, nor any alteration made in the position or use of any existing Signal, without the authority of the General Manager or the Superintendent of the Line.

Authority respecting new and altered Signals.

(*b*) Semaphore Signals not in use are distinguished by two pieces of wood nailed over each other in the form of a cross (see below) :—

Semaphore Signals not in use.

(*c*) Disc Signals not in use will not be fitted with Discs or Lamps.

Disc Signals not in use.

DEFECTIVE SIGNALS, POINTS, &c.

Defective Home, Starting, Advanced Starting, or Siding Signal.

73. (*a*) When a Home, Starting or Advanced Starting Signal, or Siding Signal applicable to a Siding not protected by Safety Points, becomes defective, or is not working efficiently, a competent person must be placed at such Signal with Hand Signals and Detonators, and act under the instructions of the Signalman. The Distant Signals applicable to the Lines affected must be kept at Danger by being disconnected from the levers by which they are worked, and must remain in that position until the defect has been made good, and all is again in working order. If the defective Signal can be placed at Danger, it must be kept at Danger until again in working order.

When Interlocking, Facing Point, Bolt, or Bar out of order.

(*b*) Should the Interlocking of a Lever-frame or any Facing Point, Bolt or Bar be out of order, one competent man or more, as may be necessary, provided with Hand Signals and Detonators, must be appointed to act under the instructions of the Signalman in charge of the Signal-box, and the Distant Signals applicable to the Lines affected must be kept at Danger by being disconnected from the levers as above directed.

Duties of Hand-signalman.

(*c*) The Hand-signalman must ascertain from the Signalman in charge of the Signal-box what train he is to bring forward, and, if the train which is to be brought forward is approaching Facing Points, he must, before signalling it forward, inform the Signalman in charge of the Signal-box the position of such Points, and satisfy himself that they are set and secured in position for the Line on which the Signalman in the Signal box intends the train should run (*d*) If the train which is to be brought forward is approaching Trailing Points, the Hand-signalman must satisfy himself that the Points are in the proper position for the train to pass.

(*e*) The Hand-signalman must, when signalling a train forward, stand near to the Signal for which he is acting, in order that his signal may not be mistaken by an Engine-driver on any other Line, and should it be necessary to stop, or reduce the speed of an approaching train, the Hand-signalman must exhibit a Red Hand Signal to the Engine-driver until the train has been stopped or the speed sufficiently reduced, and then, if permission can be given for the train to proceed, he must exhibit a Green All Right Signal held steadily in the hand.

(*f*) Hand-signalmen must work under the instructions of the Signalman only, who must take care that they are properly instructed as to their duties, and understand what they have to do.

Selection of Hand-signalmen.

(*g*) Where practicable, the Station-master must select proper men from his own staff for the purpose; but where this cannot be done he must apply to the nearest Ganger for Platelayers competent to act as Flagmen.

When Interlocking at Junction out of order.

(*h*) When the Interlocking at a Junction is out of order, the Facing Points must, except when required to be otherwise placed for the passage of trains, be so set that no train can cross the path of another train.

When Distant Signal defective.

(*i*) When a Distant Signal becomes defective, so that it cannot be placed at Danger, a competent person must be stationed just outside it with

Hand Signals and Detonators, and there repeat the Signals exhibited at the Home Signal. When such person is out of sight of the Home Signal, one man or more must be stationed between that and the defective Signal, for the purpose of repeating by Hand Signals to the man stationed at the Distant Signal the Signals exhibited at the Home Signal.

(*j*) When a Tunnel intervenes, or in foggy weather or during falling snow, the man at the Distant Signal must continue to exhibit a Hand Danger Signal, and keep two Detonators, ten yards apart, on one rail of the Line to which the Signal applies, until the Signal has been repaired and is again in working order.

(*k*) If the defective Distant Signal can be kept at Danger, it must be kept at Danger until again in working order, and a Hand-signalman need not be appointed.

When Distant or Home Signal cannot be placed at Danger.

(*l*) The Signalman at the Box in the rear must, when practicable, be advised if the Distant or Home Signal cannot be placed at Danger, and he must stop all trains proceeding in the direction of the defective Signal and advise the Engine-drivers of the circumstance.

When Fixed Signal out of order.

(*m*) When any Fixed Signal is out of order, but the Interlocking of the Point and Signal levers is in proper order, the Signalman must, to enable him to obtain the security of the Interlocking, use the lever applicable to such Signal as if the Signal were in work, and the Counter-balance weight must, when necessary, be disconnected by the Signal-fitter from the lever to admit of this being done.

74. The absence of a Signal at a place where a Signal is ordinarily shown, or a Signal imperfectly exhibited, or the exhibition of a White Light at a place where a Red or a Green Light ought to be seen, must be considered a Danger Signal, and treated accordingly, and the fact reported to the Signalman or Station-master.

Signal not shown, or imperfectly shown.

DETONATING SIGNALS.

75. (*a*) Engine-drivers, Guards, Signalmen, Gate-keepers, Gangers of Platelayers, and Fog-signalmen, must be provided with Detonators, which they must always have ready for use when on duty; and every person in charge of a Station must keep a supply of these Signals in a suitable place, known by, and easy of access at all times to, every person connected with the Station.

Supply of Detonators.

(*b*) All the persons above named will be held responsible for keeping up the proper supply of Detonators.

76. (*a*) Detonating Signals must be used for the purpose of attracting the attention of Engine-drivers. They must be placed as nearly as possible in the centre of the rail, and the clasps bent round the upper flange of the rail to prevent them from falling off.

How to be placed on rail.

(*b*) When an engine explodes a Detonator in clear weather the Engine-driver must immediately reduce speed, and bring his train under such complete control as to enable him to stop at once if required, and then proceed cautiously to the place of obstruction or until he receive a further signal for his guidance.

How Engine-driver to act on explosion of Detonator.

(*c*) When an engine explodes a Detonator in foggy weather or during falling snow the Engine-driver must immediately reduce speed, and bring his train under complete control, so as to be prepared to obey any signal that may be exhibited. If he receive a Red or Danger Hand Signal he must at once bring his train to a stand, and then proceed cautiously to the point the Hand Signal is intended to protect, or until he receive a signal to proceed, unless he be satisfied that the Hand Signal is exhibited for the purpose of repeating a Distant Signal at Danger, in which case he must, after having reduced speed, proceed cautiously towards the Home Signal. If he receive a Green Hand Signal waved slowly from side to side, he must reduce the speed of his train to fifteen miles an hour over the portion of the Line protected by such Green Signal.

(*d*) The absence of any Signal after the explosion of a Detonator must be considered equal to the exhibition of a Danger Signal.

When used to repeat Fixed Signals.

(*e*) When used to repeat Fixed Signals and call attention to the fact of their being at Danger, the Detonators must be observed in the same way that such Fixed Signals would be observed if clearly seen to be at Danger.

To be carefully handled.

77. (*a*) Detonators must be carefully handled, as they are liable to explode if roughly treated.

To be kept dry.

(*b*) They must be kept in dry places; must not be left in contact with brick walls, damp wood, or chloride of lime or other disinfectant; and must not be exposed to the action of steam or other vapour.

(*c*) Unless instructions are issued to the contrary, every man's stock of Detonators must be tested at intervals of not more than two months, to ensure that they are in good condition.

Stock to be tested.

(*d*) They must not be kept after they are three years old, or when bearing any signs of rust on the outside of the case, but must be withdrawn from the stock and returned to the Stores Department.

Not to be kept after three years old.

(*e*) Detonators must be issued in the order in which they are received from the Stores Department; those which have been the longest on hand being always used first to avoid an accumulation of old stock.

To be used in order supplied.

(*f*) Should any Detonator fail to explode when a train passes over it the circumstance must be promptly reported to the Superintendent, and the defective Detonator forwarded to him for examination.

Failure to be reported.

SIGNALLING IN FOGGY WEATHER OR DURING FALLING SNOW.

78. (*a*) In foggy weather or during falling snow it is the duty of a Station-master or other appointed person to take care that Fog-signalmen are employed at all the places where their services are required; and, where Platelayers are employed for the purpose, to arrange beforehand with the Inspector of Permanent-way the Platelayers who are to act as Fog-signalmen at the various posts. The Foreman, Ganger, or Leading Man must not be assigned a fixed Post, but must be left free to examine his road as directed by

Station-masters responsible for employing Fog-signalmen.

Rule 260. He may, however, when no other competent man is available, be employed to call the Fog-signalmen, to visit them at their Posts, and distribute Detonators and refreshments in accordance with Rules 83 and 84.

NOTE—*See modification of this Rule in Appendix to the Rule Book.*

Addresses and Posts of Fog-signalmen.

(*b*) A list of the names and addresses of the Fog-signalmen, showing the Post to which each man is appointed, must be kept exhibited in a conspicuous position in the Station-master's Office and Signal-box.

Fog or snowstorm in daytime.

79. When a fog or snowstorm occurs during the day, between 6 a.m. and 8 p.m., the men appointed to act as Fog-signalmen must at once report themselves to the Station-master, and take his instructions; those who have to do duty at Junctions or intermediate Signal-boxes away from a Station, must report themselves to the Signalmen on duty at the respective Boxes.

Employment of Fog-signalmen in the night.

80. (*a*) When it is necessary to employ Fog-signalmen during the night, between 8 p.m. and 6 a.m., the Station-master must arrange to have the men called, and sent to their respective Posts. If the Fog-signalmen become aware, from their own observation, or from information given to them, that their services are required during the night, or at any other time when off duty, they must at once report themselves to the Station-master, or to the Signalman at any Junction or intermediate Signal-box away from a Station, without waiting to be called; but this will not relieve the Station-master or Signalman from the responsibility of sending for the Fog-signalmen when necessary. If the Fog-signalman, on his way to the Signal-box to report himself for fog-signalling duty, has to pass the Signal to which he is appointed, he must, when practicable, if that Signal is at Danger, place two Detonators, ten yards apart, on one rail of the Line for which he is fog-signalling, and then proceed to the Signal-box, getting back to his Post as promptly as possible.

Fog-signalmen to get Signalman's permission before leaving duty.

(*b*) When the fog has sufficiently cleared, or the snowstorm has ceased, each Fog-signalman must place two Detonators, ten yards apart, on one rail of the Line for which he is fog-signalling, and then go to the Signalman at the Box in connection with which he is employed, and take his instructions as to whether his services are any longer required for fog-signalling duties.

NOTE.—*On some Lines only one Detonator is exploded to carry out Rules* 80, 81, 82, *and* 85, *and Engine-drivers must act in the same way as when two Detonators are exploded.*

Articles supplied to Fog-signalmen

Detail of duties.

81. (*a*) Each Fog-signalman must, before proceeding to his Post, be supplied with 36 Detonators, or more if necessary, a Hand Signal Lamp, trimmed and lighted, and a Red and a Green Flag. If fog-signalling for a Distant Signal, he must place himself outside the Signal in connection with which he works, and as far from it as is consistent with his keeping it well in sight. Whenever a train has passed him in the direction of the Signal-box from which the Signal is worked, and so long as the Signal exhibits the Danger Signal, he must place and keep two Detonators fixed, ten yards apart, on one rail of the Line for which the Signal is at Danger, and, unless instructions are issued to the contrary, exhibit a Red Hand Signal to the Engine-driver and Guard of an approaching train. When the Signal is lowered or taken off, he must remove the Detonators from the rail, and exhibit to the Engine-driver and Guard a Green Hand Signal, which must be held steadily in the hand. If he become aware of any obstruction on the Line in the immediate neighbourhood of the Signal for which he is signalling, either from a train not having gone forward, or from any other cause, he must leave the Detonators on the rail and go back along the Line, showing a Red Light with his Hand Lamp, a sufficient distance to protect such obstruction, and must there place on one rail of the Line for which he is fog-signalling three Detonators, ten yards apart, and return to within sight of the Distant Signal. When he is satisfied that the obstruction has been removed, he must take up the more distant Detonators, and return to his Post.

(*b*) The absence of any Signal after the explosion of a Detonator must be considered equal to the exhibition of a Danger Signal.

(*c*) The Fog-signalman must see that the Distant Signal which has been taken off for a train to pass is placed at Danger after the passing of such train. If, after a reasonable time has elapsed, the Signal is not placed at Danger, the Fog-signalman must go back to protect the train as above directed. The next following train must be stopped, and the Engine-driver instructed to proceed cautiously, and to inform the Signalman at the Box in advance of the circumstances. The same precautions must be taken in the event of a Distant Signal Light going out, and the Fog-signalman not being able to re-light it.

(*d*) When there is a Distant Signal Arm on a Home, Starting, or Advanced Starting Signal Post, it will not be necessary to put down more than two Detonators, although both Signals are at Danger, but the Fog-signalman must not take up the Detonators unless both Signals are lowered. Should the Home, Starting, or Advanced Starting Signal be lowered and the Distant Signal remain at Danger, the Fog-signalman must continue to exhibit his Red Hand Signal, and if the fog is so dense that the Engine-driver cannot see the Distant Signal the Fog-signalman must verbally caution him by using the words "Home Signal off—Distant on," or "Starting (or Advanced Starting) Signal off—Distant on," as the case may be.

(*e*) When a Fog-Signalman is employed in connection with Home, Starting, or Advanced Starting Signals, he must place two Detonators, ten yards apart, on one rail of the Line for which the Signal is at Danger, exhibit a Red Hand Signal to the Engine-driver of an approaching train, and carry out any instructions he may receive from the Signalman on duty.

(*f*) The Fog signalman must see that the Home, Starting, or Advanced Starting Signal which has been taken off for a train to pass is placed at Danger after the passing of such train; if, however, the Signal is not placed at Danger, the Fog signalman must, in addition to putting down two Detonators, at once communicate with the Signalman.

(*g*) After having fixed the Detonators on the rail, the Fog-signalman must place himself between the Detonators and the Fixed Signal or obstruction for which he is signalling, and so exhibit the Hand Signals that they may be seen by the Driver after the engine has exploded the Detonators.

(*h*) Fog-signalmen must stand in the best position (having regard to their own safety) for effectively giving the Hand Signals to the Engine-driver and Guard.

(*i*) When the Fixed Signal for which he is Fog-signalling cannot be seen by the Fog-signalman, he must, unless he can satisfy himself to the contrary, assume that it is at Danger.

Guards and Drivers not to rely on Fog-signalmen for protection of trains.

(*j*) In cases of accident, failure, or obstruction, Guards and Engine-drivers must act strictly in accordance with the prescribed Regulations, and must not depend upon Fog-signalmen for the protection of their trains.

NOTE.—*On some Lines only one Detonator is exploded to carry out Rules* 80, 81, 82, *and* 85, *and Engine-drivers must act in the same way as when two Detonators are exploded.*

Detonators, Hand Lamps, and Flags to be kept at Stations and in Signal boxes.

82. (*a*) A sufficient supply of Detonators, Hand Lamps, and Flags for the use of the Fog-signalmen, must be kept at the Stations and in the Signal-boxes in connection with which the men are employed. If the number of Detonators first supplied to the men is likely to become soon exhausted, they must communicate with the nearest Station or Signal-box, and obtain a further supply.

(*b*) Should the Fog-signalman have to leave his Post for this purpose, he must leave two Detonators on the rail.

NOTE.—*On some Lines only one Detonator is exploded to carry out Rules* 80, 81, 82, *and* 85, *and Engine-drivers must act in the same way as when two Detonators are exploded.*

83. (*a*) Station-masters (when the Traffic Staff is employed) or Inspectors of Permanent-way or Gangers (when Platelayers are employed) must arrange for Relief-men should the fog or snow-storm continue.

Relief-men.

(*b*) Arrangements must be made by the Station-masters for furnishing the Fog-signalmen with needful refreshments. No intoxicating liquor must be supplied to Fog-signalmen when on duty.

Refreshments for Fog-signalmen.

84. The Station-master or person in charge must satisfy himself that the Fog-signalmen have duly proceeded to their respective Posts, when it is necessary for them to do so; and, where the Fog-signalmen are numerous, a competent man must be appointed to visit them at their Posts, and see that they are properly performing their duties, and are supplied with the necessary Signals, furnishing them with a further supply of Detonators if required.

Station-master or person in charge to satisfy himself that Fog-signalmen are at their Posts.

Supply of Signals.

85. At all Signal-boxes (whether intermediate or otherwise) where no Fog-signalmen are appointed, or where such men are appointed but have not arrived, the Signalman, when he requires to stop an approaching train, in addition to keeping his Signals at Danger, must, when practicable, place two Detonators on the Line to which the Signals apply, sufficiently apart to give two distinct and separate reports.

Fog-signalling at Signal-boxes in absence of Fog-signalmen.

For Great Western practice see Rule 4 *of Block Telegraph Regulations for Double Lines in Appendix to Rule Book.*

NOTE.—*On some Lines only one Detonator is exploded to carry out Rules* 80, 81, 82, *and* 85, *and Engine-drivers must act in the same way as when two Detonators are exploded.*

Signals to be frequently worked and Apparatus examined in severe frost or falls of snow.

86. During the prevalence of severe frost or falls of snow the Signals and Points must be frequently worked by the Signalmen when the Sections are clear, and no train has been signalled, in order to prevent the frost or snow impeding their free working. Fog-signalmen also must see that nothing interferes with the true working of the Arms or Discs and Lamps of the Signals for which they are fog-signalling; that the Lamp glasses and spectacles are kept clear from snow; and that the wires work freely over the pulleys. The Fog-signalmen must at once report to the Signalman any defect in the Signals or impediment to their proper working. If no Fog-signalman is employed, the Ganger of the Permanent-way must provide for this duty being performed while the snow or frost, or its effect, continues.

STATION YARD WORKING.

Station Yard Working.

87. (*a*) Where the traffic at any Station is worked under special instructions, the Signalman, before lowering the Signals for a train to enter the Station, must satisfy himself that the special instructions have been complied with, and that the Line is clear to the point the train has to run to; but if he be in doubt, or if there be another train at the platform to which the train has to run, he must stop the train, and, except where Calling-on Arms are in use, caution the Engine-driver, both verbally and by Green Hand Signal, held steadily in the hand, before he allows it to enter the Station.

(*b*) Where the Home Signal is such a distance from the Signal-box that it is not possible for the Signalman to communicate verbally with the

Driver when the engine is standing at the Home Signal, the Signalman must, after bringing the train to a stand at the Home Signal, lower it to allow the Engine-driver to draw to his Box, and must stop the train at his Box by exhibiting a Red Flag by day and a Red Light by night. The Engine-driver must then be verbally instructed to proceed cautiously to the rear of the previous train, and a Green Flag by day and a Green Light by night, held steadily in the hand, must be exhibited by the Signalman to the Engine-driver.

Calling-on Arms.

(*c*) Where Calling-on Arms are provided, it will not be necessary to stop the train at the Signal-box, but it must, unless instructions are issued to the contrary, be brought to a stand at the Home Signal before the Calling-on Arm is lowered to allow the train to proceed as far as the Line is clear.

Engine-driver of second train to be advised before stopping.

88. At places where a train is allowed to proceed towards the rear of another train, and it is necessary, after the first train has been started, that it should be again stopped, care must be taken not to stop the Engine-driver of the first train until the Engine-driver of the second train has been advised of what is about to be done.

When second train following.

89. (*a*) When a Signal is lowered or turned off to allow a train to run upon a Line in a Station or upon a Siding, or to leave a Station or Siding, and a second train is following, the Engine-driver of the second train must follow at such a distance as will enable him to avoid colliding with the first train in the event of its being stopped, and he must bring his train to a stand at the Signal, and not pass it until it has been replaced at Danger, and again lowered or turned off.

(*b*) When a Signal is lowered or turned off to allow a second train to leave a Station or Siding to run towards a train ahead of such Signal, the Engine-driver of the second train must proceed at such a speed as to be able to stop before reaching the train ahead of the Signal.

CONTROL AND WORKING OF STATIONS.

Responsibility of Station-master or person in charge of Station.

90. (*a*) Every Station-master or person in charge of a Station is answerable for the security and protection of the office and buildings, and of the Company's property there. He is responsible for the faithful and efficient discharge of the duties devolving upon all the Company's servants, either permanently or temporarily employed at the Station, or within its limits, and such servants are subject to his authority and directions in the working of the Line. He is also responsible for the general working of the Station being carried out in strict accordance with the Company's Regulations, and must, as far as practicable, give personal attention to the shunting of trains, and all other operations which, in any way, affect the safety of the Line.

(*b*) He must also see that every servant under him connected with the working of the Line is in possession of a copy of these Rules and Regulations, and that the Working Time-tables, Appendices, and other Notices having reference to the working of the Line are properly distributed.

Station Duties.

91. Every exertion must be made for the expeditious despatch of the Station duties, and for ensuring the punctuality of the trains.

92. The Station-master must daily inspect the Station, and see that the rooms, offices, closets, urinals, and platforms are kept neat and clean. He must also take care that Station name-plates or boards, and Waiting-room or other indicators, are kept in a clean and satisfactory condition.

Daily inspection of Station.

Station and Waiting-room indicators.

93. The Station-master must see that all orders and instructions are duly entered and executed, and that all books and returns are regularly written up and neatly kept. He must also see that copies of the Company's Bye-laws, Carriers' Act, List of Fares, Statutory and other Notices, are properly exhibited at the Station and Offices

Office Duties.

94. The Station-master must report, without delay, to his superior officer, neglect of duty on the part of any of the Company's servants under his charge; and forward to him particulars of any complaint made by the public.

Neglect of duty to be reported.

95. The Station-master must be careful that all stores are prudently and economically used.

Stores.

96. The Station-master must make himself thoroughly acquainted with the duties of the Signalmen at his Station or under his control, and satisfy himself that they perform them in a proper manner, by night as well as by day; and, in order to maintain a proper supervision over the men in this respect, he must frequently visit the Signal-boxes.

Supervision of Signalmen.

97. At Signal-boxes which are switched out or closed during certain periods of the day or night the Signalman must not leave duty before the appointed time, nor until the "Train out of

Signalman leaving duty at Boxes which are switched out.

Section" signal has been received from the Box in advance for the last train he has to signal.

Note.—*See modification of this Rule in Appendix to the Rule Book.*

Safety Points and Scotches.

98. Where Safety Points are provided, care must be taken that they are always in order, and properly set to secure safety. Station-masters must see that all the Scotches are in good and sound condition; and Guards, Shunters, and others concerned must exercise great care in the securing of Vehicles in Sidings to prevent them from moving and fouling other Lines, or being blown out, or otherwise escaping on to a Running Line.

Vehicles in Sidings to be secured to prevent them from moving.

Cleaning, trimming, and lighting Signal Lamps.

99. (*a*) The greatest care must be exercised in the cleaning, trimming, and lighting of Signal Lamps, and Station-masters will be held responsible for this work being efficiently performed. The Lamps must be lighted and extinguished in accordance with Rules 67 and 116.

Trimming of Oil Burners.

(*b*) The Oil Burners of all Distant and other Fixed Signals must not be trimmed at the Signal-posts, but must be brought to the Station, Lamp-room, or Signal-box as the case may be, each morning, and cleaned and trimmed there, and not replaced in the Signal Lamps until required to be lighted.

Platform Lamps.

(*c*) The Lanterns and Reflectors of Platform Lamps must be cleaned daily, and the Oil Burners taken to the Lamp-room every morning, cleaned and trimmed, and not replaced until required.

Inspection of Signal Lamps.

(*d*) Station-masters and others having Signals under their care must frequently inspect the Fixed Signal Lamps, and satisfy themselves that they are in good working order, and that the glasses (in front and back of Lamp), spectacles and reflectors are well cleaned.

(*e*) Station-masters must see that Carriage Roof Lamps are kept clean, and properly burning when required.

Carriage Roof Lamps.

100. Luggage and parcels must not, where the width of the platform will admit, be left within six feet of the edge of the platform; barrows not in use must be kept back close to the buildings or to the wall or fence at the back of the platform, and, when necessary, so secured as to prevent them from moving.

Luggage, parcels and barrows.

101. (*a*) Platforms, crossing places, and steps of over-bridges and subways between platforms, must, when necessary, be strewn with sand, ballast, or ashes, or otherwise treated so as to avoid any cause of accident to passengers by slipping.

Platforms, steps, &c., to be sanded when necessary.

(*b*) If Station-masters have not sufficient ashes for the purpose, small ballast or sand will be supplied on application to the Inspector of Permanent-way for the district.

(*c*) During falling snow the platforms and approaches to the Stations must be kept free from snow by being carefully swept as often as necessary.

(*d*) The Permanent-way Staff must give as much assistance as possible.

102. (*a*) Each train after finishing its journey, and all vehicles shunted off at Stations as

Vehicles to be searched.

"empties" must be carefully searched, and any articles which may be found therein taken to the Station-master for instruction as to disposal.

Windows of empty compartments to be closed.

(*b*) The windows of all empty compartments must be closed, not only while the carriages are standing at Stations and Sidings, but also when the trains are running, immediately upon the compartment becoming vacant. The ventilators must be kept open.

Ventilators to be kept open.

Name of Station to be called out.

103. The Station-master must take care that immediately on the stopping of a Passenger train the name of the Station is called out along the train in a distinct and audible manner, and prompt attention must be given to any indication shown by the passengers of their desire to alight.

Doors not to be opened when train in motion.

104. (*a*) Care should be taken that the doors of all carriages and other vehicles are fastened before the train leaves the Station, and no door must be opened to allow a passenger to alight from or enter a train before it has come to a stand, or after it has started.

(*b*) Passengers showing signs of their intention to alight while a train is in motion must be requested to keep their seats till the train is brought to a stand.

Passenger train not to stop where not timed.

105. No passenger train must be stopped at a Station where it is not timed to call, for the purpose of taking up or setting down passengers, without the special authority of the General Manager or the Superintendent of the Line.

Passenger trains booked to call only when required to take up passengers.

106. In the case of a passenger train booked to call only when required to take up passengers, the necessary Fixed Signals must, when the stop has to be made, be exhibited against it; and a competent man appointed by the Station-master or person in charge must exhibit a Red Flag or Red Light from the Station platform, to intimate to the Engine-driver that his train is required to stop; such Red Flag or Red Light need not, however, be exhibited where a Fixed Signal is in such a position that a train stopped at it is at the platform.

107. (*a*) Where Carriage or Waggon Examiners are kept, the Station-master or person in charge must, before starting a train, satisfy himself that the examination of it has been completed, and that, so far as the Examiner is concerned, the train is all right, and safe to proceed.

Examination of train.

(*b*) Where Examiners are not kept steps must be taken by the Station-master or person in charge to remedy any defect which might interfere with the running of the vehicles, by supplying oil or grease to the axle-boxes of any that may require it, or removing the defective vehicles from the train, or otherwise, as may be found necessary

(*c*) The Station-master or person in charge must take care that the Break-testing and Gas-charging at Stations where such duties are performed have been completed.

108. (*a*) Examiners must, before going under vehicles, take the necessary steps to prevent the vehicles from being moved whilst the examination or other work is being performed.

Vehicles not to be moved whilst Examiners underneath

(*b*) In the event of an Examiner finding it necessary to put a "Not-to-go" label on a vehicle in a train which is marshalled and ready for starting, he must advise the Guard or Shunter what has been done.

When vehicle unfit to travel.

Use of Crane.

109. (*a*) Whenever a Crane is in use whereby the jib, or any other portion of it, obstructs or fouls any Line in use for traffic purposes, or whenever, by any possibility, during the loading or unloading of Round Timber, Long Timber, Angle Iron, or other articles of great length, any Running Line may be fouled, it is incumbent on the person in charge of the loading or unloading to obtain the sanction of both the Station-master and Signalman in charge of the safety of the Line, and to see that the proper Signals are exhibited until the operation is completed.

Loading or unloading of Round Timber, Long Timber, Angle Iron, &c.

When Crane is used at Siding not protected by Fixed Signals.

(*b*) If the Crane has to be used at a Siding not protected by Fixed Signals, a Flagman must, when necessary, be provided to protect the operation in accordance with Rule 251.

Crane to be kept locked when not in use.

(*c*) The Crane must be kept locked or otherwise secured except when actually in use.

Timber, &c., not to be loaded after dusk, or in foggy weather or during falling snow.

(*d*) After dusk, or in foggy weather or during falling snow, except where specially authorised, Timber or other articles of great length must not be allowed to be loaded or unloaded if any Running Line is liable to be fouled by the operation.

Control of Timber Loaders whilst at Stations or Sidings.

(*e*) Timber Loaders working at a Station or Siding will be under the control of the Station-master, who, whilst they are so employed, must exercise the same supervision over them as over his own staff.

Control of horses.

110. When a horse is used on the Railway a man must, on the approach, and during the passing, of any train, have hold of its head, whether the horse be drawing vehicles or not.

111. (*a*) No Engine in steam, the property of a private owner, must be allowed to enter upon any Running Line, except by the special permission of the General Manager or Superintendent of the Line.

Engines of private owners.

(*b*) Before any private engine, or Contractor's waggon, is accepted for conveyance on its own wheels, it must be examined by the Locomotive or Waggon Department, as the case may be, and the train by which it is to travel must be specially arranged. Foremen, Guards, and others concerned must satisfy themselves that this has been done before allowing the engine or waggon to travel.

Conveyance of private engine or Contractor's waggon on own wheels.

112. (*a*) Before vehicles are moved in, or shunted into, a siding used for repairing vehicles or for loading or unloading traffic, and before vehicles are moved in, or shunted into, a Goods Shed or other building where vehicles are already standing, Guards, Shunters and others concerned must take care to warn any Company's servants or other persons who may be engaged in, about, or between the vehicles; they must also request any persons who may be loading or unloading not to remain in, or near to, vehicles which are likely to be moved by shunting operations, and must satisfy themselves that no cart or other road vehicle is foul of any of the Lines on which shunting operations are about to be performed.

Men to be warned before vehicles are moved in, or shunted into Sidings, and carts or other road vehicles to be clear.

(*b*) Care must be taken to see that Goods Shed doors are open and all is clear before commencing shunting operations in the Shed Lines, and that all waggon doors are properly secured by the fastenings provided for the purpose, before being taken into, or drawn out of, the Shed, or

Shed doors to be opened and waggon doors to be secured before commencing shunting.

before being moved in, or shunted into, any Siding.

Double shunting.

113. (*a*) Double shunting is strictly prohibited, except when done by engines specially used for the purpose of shunting, attended by experienced Shunters.

Loose shunting.

(*b*) Loose shunting of vehicles against loaded Passenger trains, and of vehicles containing passengers, or live stock, or explosives, is strictly prohibited.

When vehicle has to be shunted into Siding.

(*c*) When any vehicle has to be shunted into a Siding, the Guard or Shunter must ascertain the position of the vehicles in the Siding before commencing to set back, and the Guard or Shunter must signal the Engine-driver so as to prevent the train striking the vehicles in the Siding, or the buffer-stops, with too much force.

Propping, tow-roping and chaining.

(*d*) The movement of vehicles by means of a prop or pole, or by towing with a rope or chain attached to a locomotive or vehicle moving on an adjacent line, is prohibited, except in cases where specially authorised by the Superintendent of the Line. Where special authority is given, such a means of moving a vehicle must not be resorted to except on occasions when no other reasonably practicable means can be adopted for dealing with the traffic.

At Terminal Stations.

114. At Terminal Stations, and other places where there are Dead-end Bays, after sunset and in foggy weather or during falling snow, a Red Light must be placed on the buffer-stops of arrival Lines, so as to be plainly visible to the Engine-driver of an incoming train. In the event of there being any vehicle near the buffer-stops, a Red Light must be shown on such vehicle.

115. When an accident, or obstruction of any kind, occurs on any part of the Line, it must be immediately reported by telegraph, or by the most expeditious means, to the next Station or Signal-box on each side of the place where the accident or obstruction has occurred, so that notice may be given to the Engine-drivers and Guards of approaching trains; to the Heads of Departments connected with the working of the Line; to the Locomotive Station where the Breakdown Vans for the district are kept; to the District Superintendent; to the District Engineer; to the Traffic Inspector; to the Inspector of Permanent-way; and where necessary to the Inspectors of the Signal and Telegraph Departments. It must also be reported by telegraph to those Stations where the starting of other trains is liable to be affected by the delay caused by the obstruction.

Accidents to be immediately reported.

WORKING OF LEVEL CROSSINGS.

116. (*a*) The Lamps on Level Crossing Gates must, when lighted, show a Red Light in each direction along the Line when the Gates are closed across it. The Lamps must be lighted as soon as it commences to be dusk, and in foggy weather or during falling snow.

Lighting Lamps.

(*b*) The Lamps must be extinguished in accordance with the following instructions:—At Level Crossings where a person is on duty during the night, or where a Station-master or Gatekeeper is resident on the spot, and trains are running, the Lamps must not be put out until broad daylight. At Crossings where no person is on duty during the night, nor any Station-master or Gatekeeper

Extinguishing Lamps.

is resident on the spot, or when the Line is closed during the night, the Lamps must, unless instructions are issued to the contrary, be put out before the person last on duty leaves.

(*c*) When the lamps are extinguished during the night they must, if necessary, be re-lighted for the passage of any train that may be run before daylight in the morning.

Hand Gates controlled from Signal-box.

117. Where Hand Gates are controlled from a Signal-box, the Signalman on duty must apply the controlling arrangement whenever it is necessary to prevent persons from crossing the Line.

Gates across Public Road.

118. Unless special authority be given to the contrary, the Gates must always be kept shut across the roadway, except when required to be opened to allow the Line to be crossed.

Gates not to be opened if train be near.

119. (*a*) When it is necessary for the Line to be crossed at a place which is not a Block Signal-post, the Gatekeeper must, before opening the Gates, satisfy himself that no train is near; he

Signals.

must then place his fixed Signals (where provided) at Danger to stop all coming trains, and such Signals must remain at Danger until the Line is clear, when he must close the Gates across the roadway and then take off the Signals.

(*b*) At Crossings which are Block Signal-posts, the Block Telegraph Regulations must be complied with.

Traction engines, &c. crossing Line.

120. (*a*) Traction or other heavy engines, heavy loads of timber, &c., or droves of animals, must not be allowed to cross the Railway when any train can be seen, or is known to be approaching in either direction.

(*b*) Station-masters must personally request users of Traction and other Road engines in their neighbourhood to give notice to the nearest Station-master on each occasion of their intention to pass such engines over the Railway, either at an Occupation Level Crossing or at a Public Level Crossing not provided with Fixed Signals.

(*c*) On receipt of this intimation the Station-master must arrange for a man, with Hand and Detonating Signals, to be sent out at least three-quarters of a mile from the Level Crossing in each direction to secure the safety of trains during the passage of the Traction or other engines across the Railway. If the staff at the Station will not admit of a man being sent in each direction, the services of Platelayers must be obtained.

(*d*) In the event of any person, after being warned, crossing the Railway with a Traction or other engine, at an Occupation or Public Level Crossing not provided with Fixed Signals, without giving notice to the nearest Station-master, the matter must be promptly reported to the Superintendent, with the name and address of the person so acting, in order that the case may be dealt with.

Further Gate to be first opened

121. Except at Level Crossings where the Gates on both sides of the Line are opened simultaneously, the Gate towards which road vehicles, cattle, horses, or other animals are approaching must not be opened until the opposite Gate has first been opened, so as to allow them to cross over without stopping upon the Line.

Trains to be observed as they approach and pass.

122. No Hand Signal must be given by the Gate-keeper to the Engine-driver of an approaching train if the Line is clear. He must take particular notice of each train as it approaches and passes, and, if he see anything wrong, he must show a Danger Signal to the Engine-driver and Guard, and, if necessary, exhibit his Danger Signal and place three Detonators on the rail against any following train or any train coming in the opposite direction.

Signals where Crossing is not a Block Signal-post.

123. At a Level Crossing which is not a Block Signal-post the Signals must only be used for the protection of the Crossing, or as prescribed in Rules 59, 119 and 122.

Working of Signals to be tested.

124. At Level Crossings where Fixed Signals are provided the Gatekeeper must test their working both by day and by night. Gatekeepers and others in charge of Gates, Signals or Points, must give notice to the Inspector of Permanent-way, Foreman Platelayer, Ganger, or other person in charge of repairs, immediately any repairs are required thereto; if any part become defective or broken, or should any Gate not close properly and fasten itself on the instant of its being shut, they must immediately request the nearest Plate-layer to have the same put right, and the matter must be reported to the nearest Station-master.

Defects to be reported.

TRAIN SIGNALS.

Distinctive Head Lamps, Discs, and Boards.

125. For the information of Station-masters, Signalmen, and others, each engine must carry the prescribed Head Lamps or Discs, and Destination Boards where provided.

Tail Lamp to indicate last vehicle.

126. Every train travelling on the Line must have a Tail Lamp, properly cleaned and trimmed, attached to the last vehicle, by day as well as by night. The Lamp need not be lighted in the daytime, except in foggy weather or during falling snow, or where otherwise provided, but its presence in the rear of each passing train will furnish evidence to the Signalmen that no portion of the train has become detached.

127. (*a*) After sunset, and in foggy weather or during falling snow, every engine must carry the necessary Head Lights, and, when running alone, a Red Tail Light also; and except as shown in the following paragraph, or where instructions are issued to the contrary, every train while on any Running Line must carry a Red Tail Light on the last vehicle, and two Red Side Lights.

Tail, Side, and Head Lights, after sunset and in foggy weather or falling snow.

(*b*) Where trains are run in the same direction on Parallel Lines, special Regulations for Head, Side and Tail Lamps will be made, when necessary, to meet the circumstances of each case.

Head, Side, and Tail Lamps on Parallel Lines.

NOTE—*For details of the practice to be observed, see Appendix to the Rule Book.*

(*c*) The Guard, if there be only one, or the rear Guard, if there be more than one, must see that the Tail and Side Lamps are kept properly burning when necessary.

Guard to see that Tail and Side Lamps are burning.

128. (*a*) Engines when on any Running Line without a train must carry a Tail Lamp in the rear both by day and by night.

Engine Tail Lamp.

(*b*) Engines assisting trains in the rear must carry a Tail Lamp.

(*c*) Engines drawing trains must not carry any Tail Lamp in the rear.

(*d*) In the case of two or more engines running coupled together without a train, the last engine only must carry a Tail Lamp.

129. Shunting engines employed exclusively in Station Yards and Sidings must, after sunset or in foggy weather or during falling snow, carry both

Shunting engines.

Head and Tail Lamps showing a Red Light or such other Light as may be prescribed.

Specials following.

130. (*a*) An additional Tail Lamp or a Red Board or a Red Flag by day, or an additional Red Tail Light by night, carried on the last vehicle of a train or on an engine, indicates that a Special train is to follow; but the additional Tail Signal need not be carried by preceding trains for Special trains of which previous printed or written notice has been given.

Specials run under notice.

Specials run without notice.

(*b*) A printed or written notice of Special trains must be given when practicable, but when such trains have to run at short notice, and the issue of a printed or written advice is impossible, the train must be telegraphed from the starting point to the necessary Stations in advance. The staff must at all times be prepared for extra trains.

Special Passenger train following.

(*c*) The Station-master or person in charge at the starting point of a Special Passenger train, of the running of which no previous printed or written notice has been given, must, when practicable, take care that the additional Tail Signal is affixed on the last vehicle of the preceding train, and he must inform the Guard in charge of it of the description and destination of the Special train. The Guard of the train preceding the Special train must inform the person in charge of each Station at which he stops of the description and destination of the train that is following, and take care that the additional Tail Signal is removed from his own train when no longer wanted.

Relief trains.

(*d*) Relief trains, if run without previous printed or written notice, must be considered and treated as Special trains.

131. (*a*) When Slip carriages are run on a train the indications must be as follow :—

Slip carriage Signals.

If there be only one slip portion.

One Red and one White Tail Light placed side by side on the rear of the Slip portion, thus :—

RED WHITE

If there be two separate Slip portions on the same train.

One Red and one White Tail Light placed vertically on the rear of the portion first to be slipped, thus:—

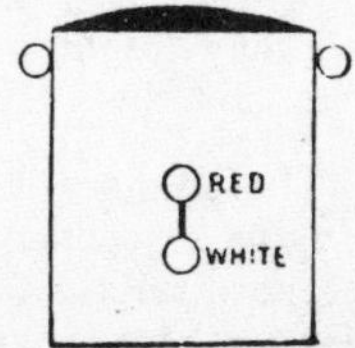

One Red and one White Tail Light placed side by side on the second or inner Slip portion, thus :—

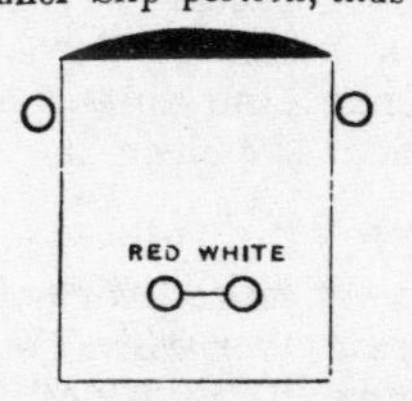

By day the Lamps must be encircled by Discs of the same colour as the Lights shown by night.

White Head Light to be carried on Slip portion.

(*b*) The Slip portion, or the first carriage where there is more than one to be slipped at the same Station, must, after dusk and in foggy weather or during falling snow, carry a White Head Light, in order that after the Slip portion has been detached, Signalmen and others may see it approaching.

NOTE.—*In addition to the Tail Lamps, as above, each set of "Slips" must carry the usual Side Lights.*

For Regulations for Working Slip Carriages, see Appendix to the Rule Book.

WORKING OF TRAINS.

Time of attendance.

132. The Engine-driver and Fireman must be with their Engine at such time previous to the starting of the train as the Locomotive Superintendent may require, and they must satisfy themselves that their Engine is in proper order.

Engine to be in proper order.

Articles to be taken.

133. The Engine-driver must have with him on his Engine or tender a complete set of Lamps, a box of not less than twelve Detonators, two Red Flags, a Fire-bucket, and such tools as may be ordered by the Locomotive Superintendent.

Engine not to be in motion on Running Line without Driver and Fireman being upon it.

134. Except where otherwise provided, no engine must be allowed to be in motion on any Running Line unless both the Engine-driver and Fireman are upon it.

Driver and Fireman not to leave engine.

135. The Driver and Fireman, when on duty, must not leave their engine unless it is absolutely necessary for them to do so, nor, except as directed in the Rules, without a man being left in charge of it or the engine is in a siding and out of gear with the Hand-break hard on.

136. The Engine-driver and Fireman, before commencing duty, must ascertain from the Notices posted for their guidance if there be anything requiring their special attention on those parts of the Line over which they have to work.

Notices to be examined before commencing duty.

137. The Engine-driver and Fireman must take care that the coal on the tender is not stacked too high, and that it and the boxes, fire-irons, and tools which are carried on the tender are so placed that they will not fall off when the engine is in motion.

Coal, &c., to be safely placed on tenders.

138. If an Engine-driver is not thoroughly acquainted with any portion of the Line over which he has to run, he must obtain the services of a Pilot-driver.

When Engine-driver not acquainted with Line.

139. The Engine-driver must keep a good look-out all the time the engine is in motion, and the Fireman must also do so, when he is not necessarily otherwise engaged.

Engine-driver to keep a good look-out.

140. After the Station work is completed Engine-drivers must not move their trains forward toward the Starting Signal before it is lowered, except when they are specially ordered to do so by the Station-master or person in charge.

Not to move train towards Starting Signal until lowered.

141. No engine must enter upon, set back from, or cross, any Running Line without the permission of the person in charge of the Points and Signals, nor then until the proper Signals have been exhibited.

Engine not to foul Running Line without permission, and proper Signals.

142. The Engine-driver must, before starting, see that the proper Engine Destination Boards (where provided), Discs, and Lamps are exhibited, and are in good order, and that the Lamps are lighted and kept burning when necessary.

Engine Destination Boards, Discs, and Lamps to be in good order.

In foggy weather or during falling snow speed to be reduced if Fixed Signals are not visible.

143. The Engine-driver and Fireman must carefully observe all Signals, and when, from fog or falling snow, or from any other cause, the Fixed Signals are not visible as soon as usual, the speed must be reduced, and every possible precaution used, especially in approaching Stations and Junctions, so that they may be able to stop the train short of any obstruction, should the Signals be against them.

Driver to travel cautiously, and to stop if Fixed or Hand Signals cannot be seen.

144. In foggy weather or during falling snow the Engine-driver must travel cautiously, keeping a sharp look-out for the Fog-signalmen, who will, if the Signals are off, show him a Green Hand Signal held steadily in the Hand. When the fog is so dense that the Fixed Signals cannot be seen by the Engine-driver on approaching or passing them, he must, unless he see the Fog-signalman's Green Hand Signal, assume that the Fixed Signal is at Danger, and act in accordance with Rule 74

To regulate speed.

145. (*a*) The Engine-driver must regulate the running of his engine as accurately as practicable, according to the Working Time-table, so as to avoid extreme speed, or loss of time.

Speed of Special trains.

(*b*) Special trains not timed must be run as nearly as practicable at the same rate of speed as corresponding trains shown in the Working Time-table, and of which they may form a part; and the speed of Special trains must not exceed that of such corresponding trains, unless under specific instructions from the Superintendent of the Line.

To observe and obey Signals.

146. The Engine-driver and Fireman must pay immediate attention to and obey all Signals, whether the cause of the Signal being shown is known to them or not. The Engine-driver must not, however, trust entirely to Signals, but must be vigilant and cautious. He must also obey the instructions of the officers in charge of Stations.

To be vigilant and cautious.

147. (*a*) As far as practicable, the Engine-driver must have his Fireman disengaged when approaching or passing a Signal-box, so that he also may keep a good look-out for Signals.

Fireman to look out.

(*b*) When approaching a Junction the Engine-driver must give the required notice by whistle if the Signals are at Danger; if the proper signals are lowered for him to proceed, he need not give the Junction whistles.

Junction whistles.

148. (*a*) Engine-drivers of trains, when running through Junctions to or from Lines diverging from the straight road, must so reduce their speed as to ensure a steady passage for the whole train through the Junction Points and Crossings.

Speed of trains when passing through Junction Points and Crossings.

(*b*) Where special rates of speed are to be observed in running over certain Junctions and other portions of the Line, they will be found in the Notices or Appendices.

Special rates of speed.

149. (*a*) When one or more engines are employed to assist a train in the rear, they must not, unless authorised by the General Manager or the Superintendent of the Line, leave the train except at a Block Signal-box where there is a Signalman on duty.

Assistant engine not to leave train except at Signal-box.

(*b*) When a Goods train is assisted by an engine in the rear the Guard must remove his Tail Lamp, and when the assisting engine leaves the train the Tail Lamp must, when practicable, be

Goods train assisted by engine in rear.

replaced within view of the Signalman, to remind him that an assisting engine is following, and in order to prevent the train being signalled to the Box in advance as having passed without a Tail Lamp. Should the assisting engine, from any cause, leave the train between two Signal boxes, and the train proceed without it, the Guard must take care not to replace the Tail Lamp until the train has passed out of sight of the Signalman at the next Box, and he must use every endeavour to intimate to the Signalman at such Box that the assisting engine has been left on the Line.

Starting of trains with one engine in front and one in rear of train.

(*c*) When the Driver of the Engine in front has received the Guard's signal to start, and he has satisfied himself that the necessary Fixed Signal has been lowered, he must call the attention of the Driver in the rear of the train by giving two "Crow" whistles, which must be acknowledged by repetition from the rear engine, and until these "Crows" have been given and acknowledged, neither the train engine nor the assisting engine must move forward.

(*d*) When two or more engines are employed to draw a train they must not be uncoupled except at a Block Signal-box where there is a Signalman on duty, nor then until the engines have been brought to a stand.

Light engines to be coupled.

(*e*) When two or more light engines have to pass at the same time through a Block Section they must be coupled together before entering such Section. The Continuous Break Pipes, where provided, must also be coupled, and the engines must not be uncoupled except at a Block Signal-Box where there is a Signalman on duty.

(*f*) When it may be necessary to detach one engine from another on any Running Line, the Driver of each engine requiring to be detached must, before uncoupling, verbally communicate with the Signalman and make him clearly understand what is about to be done, and in what direction the uncoupled engine or engines are required to proceed.

Detaching One engine from another on Running Line.

EXCEPTION.—*When a Passenger train worked by two engines is brought to a stand at a Station, and one has to be detached during the time the train is at the platform, it will not be necessary, before uncoupling the engine, for the Engine-driver to communicate with the Signalman, but after the engine has been uncoupled, the Driver must, if the engine has to run to a Signal-box in advance before being placed clear of the Running Lines, or otherwise disposed of, at once inform the Signalman there what has been done.*

149A. (*a*) To facilitate the working of traffic two Goods or Mineral trains may, in clear weather (and where specially authorised by the General Manager or the Superintendent of the line), be coupled together, the engine of the second train being coupled to the break-van of the first train, and the two trains worked forward as one train.

Coupling Goods or Mineral Trains together.

(*b*) At places where such special authority is given the Signalman must decide as to the coupling of trains together, and before the engine of the second train is attached to the break van of the first train, the Guard of the first train must satisfy himself that the Driver of his own train is aware of what is about to be done.

(*c*) When the Engine-driver in front has received his Guard's Signal to start, and he has satisfied himself that the necessary Fixed Signal has been lowered, he must call the attention of the Driver of the second train by giving two "Crow" whistles, which must be acknowledged by repetition from the rear engine, and until these "Crows" have been given and acknowledged, neither engine must move forward, and the Guard of the first train must not give the Signal to start until he has exchanged Signals with the Guard and Driver of the second train.

(*d*) The Tail and Side Lamps at the rear of the first train must be removed as soon as the trains are coupled together, and must not be replaced until the trains are again divided, which must not be done until the coupled trains have been brought to a stand at a Signal-box, when the engine of the second train must be uncoupled from the break-van of the first train by the Head Guard of the first train, and the Tail and Side Lamps must be replaced by him in their proper positions.

(*e*) When trains are coupled together they must be signalled specially, as may be arranged, and the Signalmen, after receiving such special signal, must not give the "Train out of Section" signal to the Signal-box in the rear until both trains have passed out of the section.

(*f*) Coupled trains must not be sent to any Station or Siding unless it is known that they can be dealt with there.

(*g*) The Guard of each train must ride in the break-van at the rear of his own train.

(*h*) On Lines where the absolute Block Telegraph System is not in operation, when a train is standing outside the Home Signal and a following train arrives behind it, the Guard in charge of the first train must confer with the Driver of the second train, and if both trains are going in the same direction and they can be coupled for a part or the whole of the journey, the Guard of the first train must take the instructions of the Signalman on duty as to whether the trains should be coupled or not.

(*i*) On falling gradients Guards of the coupled trains must apply the Hand-breaks in sufficient time to keep the couplings tight when the trains commence to ascend the next rising gradient.

(*j*) When either of the Drivers of the coupled trains finds it necessary to stop he must give three or more short sharp whistles, or sound the break-whistle (where a special whistle is supplied for that purpose) as a signal to the other Driver to shut off steam and apply his Break.

(*k*) In foggy weather or during falling snow, trains must not be coupled together, but must be worked separately.

Train drawn by two engines.

150. (*a*) When two engines are employed to draw a train the Driver and Fireman of the leading engine are responsible for the observance of Signals and the working of the Continuous Break; the Driver of the second engine must watch for, and take his Signals from, the Driver of the leading engine, but the Driver of the second engine is not relieved from the due observance of all Signals regulating the safe working of the Line, and in case of need he must apply the Continuous Break.

Duty of each Engine-driver as to Signals.

Care in starting or stopping.

(*b*) Special care must be used in starting or stopping a train drawn by two engines to prevent the breaking of the couplings.

To start and stop with care.

To run on proper Line.

151. (*a*) The Engine-driver must start and stop his train carefully and without a jerk, and pass along the proper Line, which, in the case of an ordinary double Line, is the left-hand side of the Permanent-way, in the direction in which the engine is travelling.

Stopping of trains.

(*b*) In stopping his train he must pay particular attention to the state of the weather and the condition of the rails, as well as to the length and weight of the train; and these circumstances must have due consideration in determining when to shut off the steam and to apply the Break.

To be careful in approaching Stations, and not to stop short of, or over-run, platform.

152. (*a*) The Engine-driver must carefully approach all Stations at which his train is required to stop, and must not stop short of, or over-run, the platform; he must also exercise care in passing Stations where he is not required to stop.

When a Passenger train over-runs, or stops short of, platform.

(*b*) Should a Passenger train in stopping at a Station, over-run, or stop short of, the platform, the Engine-driver must not move the train back or draw it forward until he receives instructions from the Guard in charge to do so. Station-masters, Guards, and others must at once take steps to prevent passengers leaving the carriages that are not at the platform; and as soon as the Guard in charge has satisfied himself that all doors are closed, and that no passengers are entering or leaving the train, he must instruct the Engine-driver to put back or draw up to the platform as may be required. The Engine-driver must sound his whistle before moving his train.

(*c*) In the event of the whole of the train running past the platform and out of sight of the Signalman, the Guard must not give instructions to the Driver to set the train back without the authority of the Signalman.

Trains stopped where not booked to call.

(*d*) Should a Passenger train be stopped by Signals at a Station platform where it is not booked to call, the Engine-driver must not, on the Signal being lowered, proceed without receiving an All Right Signal from the Guard.

Use of whistle.

153. Should a train be approaching, stopping at, or leaving a Station, on the opposite Running Line, or should shunting operations be going on, the Engine-driver must, on approaching and whilst passing, sound the engine whistle. The whistle must also be sounded to caution Platelayers at work on or near the Line on which a Train is running, and on entering a Tunnel to warn all men at work inside, and must be repeated occasionally when passing through long Tunnels. Engine-drivers must not throw out hot water, fire, or cinders when passing through a Tunnel.

Whistle to warn men, and on entering and passing through Tunnels.

Engine-driver not to throw out hot water, &c., in Tunnels.

Train at stand on opposite Line obscured by steam or smoke.

154. Should an Engine-driver observe a train or an Engine at a stand on the opposite Line to that on which he is travelling obscured by steam or smoke, he must sound his whistle and approach it very cautiously, so as to be able to stop if necessary.

Platelayers' Signals to reduce speed.

155. A Green Flag or a Green Light, waved slowly from side to side by Platelayers, indicates that trains must reduce speed to fifteen miles an hour, or such other speed as may be prescribed, over the portion of Line protected by such Green Signal.

Engine not to stand foul of Points or Crossings.

156. When a Driver brings his engine to a stand in obedience to Signals, he must take care that the engine does not stand foul of the Points or Crossings of any other Running Line.

Catch Points.

157. (*a*) Unless instructions are issued to the contrary, or in the event of an obstruction being in front, no train must be brought to a stand where there are Catch Points until the last vehicle has passed over such Catch Points.

(*b*) If a train is brought to a stand on or near Catch Points the Engine-driver must not move his train until he has satisfied himself that the Points are in the proper position, and that all is right for the train to be moved.

Hose of Water Tanks to be properly secured.

158. Engine-drivers, after taking water from Tanks or Water Columns, must be careful to leave the Hose or Water Crane clear of the Running Lines and properly secured.

Smoke from Engines.

159. Engine-drivers and Firemen must so arrange their fires as to avoid any unnecessary emission of smoke from their engines whilst standing at or passing Stations.

Engine-driver to assist in forming train.

Train under control of Head Guard.

160. The Engine-driver must afford such assistance with his engine as may be required for the formation, arrangement, and despatch of his train. Each train is under the control of the Head Guard, who must give the Engine-driver any instructions that may be necessary as to the working of the train.

161. Every Guard must be in attendance at the Station from which he is to start half an hour before the time appointed for the departure of his train, or at such other time as may be specially fixed.

Attendance of Guard prior to departure of train.

162. Every Guard, before starting with his train, must examine the Notices to see whether there is anything requiring his special attention on those parts of the Line over which he has to work, and he must, before going off duty, ascertain the time at which he is again required to be on duty.

Guards to examine Notices.

163. Every Passenger Guard must have with him his Watch, Whistle, and Carriage Key, and take in his van a Red and a Green Flag, not less than twelve Detonators, a Hand Signal Lamp, which must be lighted before passing through long Tunnels and after sunset and in foggy weather, and such other Articles or Flags as may be ordered by the Superintendent of the Line.

Articles a Passenger Guard to have with him.

164. Every Goods Guard must have with him his Watch, and take with him in his van a Red and a Green Flag, not less than twelve Detonators, a Hand Signal Lamp, which must be lighted before passing through long Tunnels and after sunset and in foggy weather, a Shunting Pole, not less than two Sprags, and such other Articles or Flags as may be ordered by the Superintendent of the Line.

Articles a Goods Guard to have with him.

NOTE.—*See addition to this Rule in Appendix to the Rule Book.*

165. The Guard in charge of a Passenger train must satisfy himself before starting that the train is correctly formed, labelled and provided with the necessary lamps; that the vehicles are properly coupled; and that the Continuous Break is in working order.

Duties of Head Guard.

Doors to be closed.

Unusual stoppage.

166. Guards must see that the doors of the carriages and other vehicles are properly closed and fastened, and, in case of any unusual stoppage, must request the passengers to keep their seats, except when necessary to alight.

Preventing passengers travelling in superior class.

Re-booking by same train prohibited.

Fraudulent travelling.

167. Guards must assist the Staff at Stations in preventing passengers travelling in a superior class, or leaving a train for the purpose of re-booking by the same train to evade payment of the proper fare; and they must also assist the Staff generally in detecting fraudulent travelling.

Guards under orders of Station-master.

168. When trains are within Station limits the Guards are under the orders of the Station-master or person in charge.

Packages not to be conveyed unless booked.

Guards to compare parcels with way-bills.

169. Guards and other servants of the Company are forbidden to carry any description of package, either for themselves, their friends, or the public, without proper authority in writing for the free transit thereof, or unless such package be properly entered on a way-bill. Passenger Guards must compare the parcels with the way-bills, and note on the latter any defect or discrepancy. All way-bills must be initialled or stamped by the Guards.

Guards to keep a good Look-out.

Luggage, parcels, &c.

170. (*a*) Guards of Passenger trains must, as far as practicable, keep a good Look-out ahead, and be prepared to take any action that may be necessary. They must also give prompt attention to the luggage, parcels, despatches, and other packages entrusted to them. Parcels which have to be put out must be given by the Guard to the

Porter appointed to receive them, who must sign in the Guard's book for the value parcels delivered to him. The Guard must, in like manner, sign in the Porter's book for the value parcels transferred to his care.

(*b*) On the arrival of the train at a terminus the Guards must not leave until they have delivered over all luggage and parcels, together with the way-bills relating thereto, to the persons appointed to take charge of them, and care must be taken not to allow any unauthorised person to enter a break-van or luggage compartment; should any article be missing, the Guards must immediately report the case to the person in charge of the Station and on their journals.

Guards not to leave Station until they have delivered over parcels and luggage.

171. (*a*) No Passenger train must be started before the time stated in the Time-table.

Starting of Passenger trains.

(*b*) The Signal for starting a Passenger train must be given by the Guard showing a Hand Signal, and, when necessary, blowing his whistle, after obtaining an intimation from the Station-master, or person in charge, that all is right for the train to proceed.

If a Flag is used in the day time as the Signal to start it must be a Green one; at night, when a Lamp is used as the Signal, it must show a Green Light, and be held steadily above the head.

(*c*) When there are two or more Guards the Signal to the Engine-driver to start must be given by the Guard nearest the engine after he has exchanged Signals with the Guard or Guards in the rear, who must first have received intimation from the Station-master or person in charge that all is right for the train to proceed.

(*d*) The intimation from the Station-master, or person in charge, that all is right for the train to proceed must be a Hand Signal by day, and when the Signal is given by Hand Lamp it must be a White Light held steadily above the head.

(*e*) Should a Passenger train be stopped by an accident or from any other exceptional cause the Engine-driver must not again start until he has exchanged Hand Signals with the Guard, or in the case of more than one Guard, not until he has received a Signal from the Guard nearest the engine, who must first exchange Hand Signals with the Guard in the rear.

Starting of Goods trains.

(*f*) Goods trains may be run before the time specified in the Time-table, provided the Line on which they have to run, and the Stations and Sidings at which they are booked to stop, will be open and ready for traffic purposes by the time they arrive, and that the next Station or Shunting Siding can be reached without causing delay to following trains of more importance.

(*g*) The Signal for starting a Goods train must, by day, be given by the Guard holding one arm in a horizontal position, and at night by a Hand Lamp showing a Green Light held steadily above the head.

When there are two or more Guards the Signal to the Engine-driver to start must be given by the Guard nearest the Engine after he has exchanged Signals with the Guard or Guards in the rear.

(*h*) At the commencement of the journey, or when re-starting from a Station, Goods Yard, Siding or Signal, or after being stopped from any exceptional cause, the Engine-driver must, as soon as practicable after the train has started, satisfy himself that his Fireman has exchanged Hand Signals with the Guard in the rear, so that the Engine-men may be sure that they have the Guard and the whole of the train with them. A short whistle will, if necessary, gain the attention of the Guard for the purpose.

Not to leave Station, Siding, or Ticket Platform without proper Signal.

172. (*a*) When a train is about to leave a Station, Siding, or Ticket Platform, the Signal to start given by the Guard merely indicates that the Station duty or the collection of tickets is completed; and, before starting the train, the Engine-driver must satisfy himself that the Line is clear, either by observation, or the exhibition of the necessary Signal; when starting, the Fireman must look back to see that the whole of the train is following in a safe and proper manner, and to receive any Signal from the Station-master or Guard that may be necessary.

Engine-driver and Fireman to look back.

(*b*) The Engine-driver and Fireman must frequently during the journey, especially when passing a Signal-box, look back and see that the whole of the train is following in a safe and proper manner.

Goods trains to stop as marked in Time-table.

173. Goods trains must stop at the places specified in the Time-table, unless, on approaching a Station or Siding, the Fixed Signals are off for the train to proceed, and a Green Hand Signal, waved slowly up and down, is given to indicate that it is not necessary for the train to stop.

Exceptions.

When this is done the train may run past the Station or Siding without stopping, unless there are waggons or goods to leave, when the Engine-driver will have instructions from the Guard to stop. In the case of a train timed to stop at a Station or Siding when required, the Engine-

Goods trains timed to stop when required.

driver of such train must stop at the Station or Siding, unless he receive a Green Hand Signal, waved slowly up and down, to proceed without stopping.

Coupling of carriages.

174. (*a*) To prevent oscillation, and to secure the smooth and easy running of Passenger trains, all the vehicles composing the train must be so tightly coupled as to put sufficient strain on the drawbars to ensure the buffers being brought so firmly together as not to be separated by any change of gradient or by the starting of the train.

Side chains.

(*b*) Side chains, where provided, must always be coupled, and the screw coupling not in use must be hung on the hook provided for the purpose.

Station-masters at intermediate Stations to examine couplings.

(*c*) Station-masters at intermediate Stations must, as far as practicable, observe the state of the couplings (including Continuous Break, Passenger Communication, and other couplings) on the arrival of the trains, and cause any that require it to be adjusted.

Information as to running of trains.

175. (*a*) Station-masters and Signalmen must, when necessary, ascertain how the Ordinary and Special trains in their respective districts are running.

Passenger trains to take precedence.

(*b*) Passenger trains must, as a rule, take precedence of all other trains.

Shunting of trains for others to pass.

(*c*) Goods trains must be shunted out of the way of Passenger trains; and Mineral, Slow Goods, and Ballast trains must also be shunted out of the way of Fast Goods, Cattle, and Fish trains at Stations or Sidings where there are fixed Signals, in sufficient time to prevent the Passenger train, Fast Goods, Cattle, or Fish train, respectively, being delayed by the Signals either at the

Station where the train is being shunted or at the Station in the rear.

(*d*) Wherever there is sufficient Siding accommodation to contain the train it must not be shunted from one Running Line to another, but always from the Running Line into the Siding.

176. When the last vehicle of a train does not pass the Signal-box before it has been shunted into a Siding, or when a train has been brought to a stand within the Home Signal, and it is necessary to give the "Train out of Section" Signal before the train passes the Signal-box, the Signalman must, before giving such Signal, ascertain from the Guard or Shunter in charge of the train that the whole of the train, with Tail Lamp attached, has arrived, and the Guard or Shunter will be held responsible for giving this information to the Signalman, the Fireman being similarly responsible in the case of a light engine.

When last vehicle of train does not pass Signal-box before it has been shunted into a Siding.

177. (*a*) The Guard must ride in his break-van and not in any other part of the train or upon the engine, except when required to do so in the execution of his duty.

Guard to ride in break-van.

(*b*) He must keep a good Look-out, and should he see any reason to apprehend danger he must use his best endeavours to give notice thereof to the Engine-driver. If the train is fitted with the Continuous Break he must, in case of emergency, apply it in order to stop the train. If the train is not fitted with the Continuous Break he must apply his Hand-break sharply, and release it suddenly. This operation repeated several times is almost certain, from the check it occasions, to attract the notice of the Engine-driver, to whom the necessary Danger Signal must be exhibited.

To keep a good Look-out.

Means to be adopted by Guard to attract Engine-driver's attention.

Means to be adopted by Engine-driver to attract Guard's attention.

(*c*) In the case of trains not fitted with the Continuous Break, the Guard must always apply his Break as soon as he becomes aware that the Engine-driver is applying his.

When, however, an Engine-driver requires the special assistance of the Guard's break, he must give three or more short, sharp whistles, or sound the Break-whistle (when a special whistle is supplied for that purpose), and the Guard or Guards must immediately apply the breaks.

Guards to apply Hand-break when necessary.

178. In travelling down steep inclines Guards of Goods trains must, in order to steady the trains and assist the Engine-drivers, apply the rear Hand-break, care being taken not to skid the wheels; they must also, where necessary, fasten down a sufficient number of waggon-breaks before descending the incline. Guards must apply their breaks when a train is approaching, at too great a speed, a Station at which it is timed to stop.

Engine not to push train.

179. Except as shown below, no engine must push a train upon any Running Line, but must draw it.

Exceptions.

Exceptions.—

(*a*) When within Station limits or where specially authorised by the General Manager or the Superintendent of the Line.

(*b*) Under special regulations when assisting up inclines.

(*c*) When a train or portion of a train is left upon any Running Line, and the engine returns for it upon the proper Line, and crosses behind it, as shown in Rule 221.

(*d*) When a train has to return on the wrong Line to the Signal-box in the rear, as shown in Rule 222.

(*e*) In the case of an engine being disabled a following engine may push the train slowly to the next Siding or Crossover road (see Block Telegraph Rule 14), when the pushing engine must go in front.

(*f*) When the Line is blocked, and trains are being worked to the point of obstruction, on both sides.

(*g*) Engines of Ballast trains when working in a Section, unless instructions are given to the contrary.

(*h*) When required to assist in starting a train from a Station.

(*i*) When required by Officers of the Company travelling in an inspection carriage by Special train.

Detaching vehicles from Passenger train.

180. (*a*) When any vehicle has been detached from a Passenger train, the Guard must, unless some of the Station staff are present to take charge of it, see that it is properly secured so as to prevent its moving. If the engine be detached to put off or take on vehicles, or for any other purpose, the Guards must keep their Hand-breaks on to prevent the train moving during the time the engine is away from it.

Detaching vehicles from Passenger train.

(*b*) The Continuous Break must not be relied upon to secure any vehicle from running away after it has been detached from the engine and break-van.

Attaching and detaching vehicles of Goods train where Line is not level.

181. When a Goods train has been brought to a stand on any Running Line, where the Line is not level and it is necessary for the engine to be detached from the train to attach or detach waggons, or for any other purpose, the Guard must, before the engine is uncoupled, satisfy himself that the van-breaks have been put on securely; and, as an additional precaution, he must pin down a sufficient number of waggon-breaks, and place one or more sprags in the wheels of the waggons next to the rear break in the case of a rising gradient, and of the foremost waggons in the case of a falling gradient, so as to prevent the possibility of the waggons moving away. The number of sprags must be regulated by the steepness of the gradient, the number of waggons, their loads, and the state of the weather and rails.

Shunting of train into Siding or from one Running Line to the other to allow another to pass.

182. (*a*) When a train is shunted into a siding after sunset, or in foggy weather or during falling snow, for another train to pass, the Tail and Side Lamps must be removed or so disposed of as not to exhibit the Red Lights to a following train.

(*b*) When a train has to be shunted from one Running Line to another to allow a following train to pass, such train must be set well within the Home Signal, so as to be efficiently protected by it from any train approaching from the opposite direction.

(*c*) Before any train is shunted from one Running Line to another after sunset, or in foggy weather or during falling snow, the Engine-driver must exhibit a Red Head Light in front of the engine (or tender if running tender first), so as to face a train coming from the opposite direction, and remove all other Head Lights which his engine may be carrying. The Red Light must be kept exhibited until the whole of the shunted train has again been placed on its proper Running Line.

(*d*) Immediately a train has been shunted from one Running Line to another the Guard (in the case of a train) must remove the Tail Light and reverse or obscure the Side Lights, and the Engine-driver (in the case of a light engine) must remove the Tail Light.

(*e*) Before the train recrosses to its proper Running Line the Guard (in the case of a train) must replace the Tail and Side Lights, and the Engine-driver (in the case of a light engine) must replace the Tail Light.

Detaching engine from train standing on wrong Line.

(*f*) Should it be necessary for the engine to be detached and leave its train standing on the wrong Line, the Guard in charge must place a Red Light on the front vehicle of the train so left, and the Engine-driver will be held responsible for seeing that this is done before removing his engine from the train.

(*g*) Should the engine have to remove a portion of the train, the Guard in charge must see that a Red Light, as above, is left exhibited on the front vehicle of the rear portion before the front portion is removed.

(*h*) In the case of a train or vehicles having to be shunted from a Siding on to a Running Line or from one Running Line to another Running Line, and having to stand there, the Shunter or other person in charge must, after sunset, or in foggy weather or during falling snow, take care that a Red Light is placed on the end of the train or vehicles so as to face any train that may be approaching on the same line.

Shunting operations.

183. During shunting operations an Engine-driver must not move his train, although the Fixed Signal may be lowered, until he has received a Hand Signal to do so from the Guard, Shunter, or other person in charge.

Shunting waggons.

184. (*a*) Waggons must not be shunted into Sidings, nor against other waggons upon Running Lines, without remaining attached to the engine, unless the waggons are attended by a competent person prepared to put down the waggon-breaks, or to apply sprags, as the case may be, so as to prevent their coming into violent contact with other waggons or vehicles, or fouling other Lines, or running away when the Line is on a falling gradient.

(*b*) Waggons must not be moved unless the doors are properly closed and fastened.

Waggons left standing in Sidings.

(*c*) Waggons left standing in Sidings must be clear of the fouling points of any adjoining Sidings or Lines, and properly secured to admit of shunting operations being carried on without risk of injury to the staff engaged in conducting them.

Shunting waggons into incline Sidings.

(*d*) When waggons have to be shunted into incline Sidings, the waggons to be moved at one shunt must be limited to such a number as the engine can push up without going at a violent or excessive speed.

(*e*) When shunting waggons at Stations or other places situate on inclines, care must be taken that, in addition to screwing the van-breaks tightly down, a sufficient number of waggon-breaks are fastened down, and sprags or hand-scotches used when necessary, to prevent the possibility of the train or any of the vehicles running down the incline. At such Stations and at such other places a supply of sprags and hand-scotches must be kept ready for the purpose.

Shunting waggons at Stations on inclines—waggons to be secured.

Sprags and hand-scotches to be kept at Stations.

185. (*a*) Guards and Shunters performing shunting operations at Sidings must take care that the vehicles are left clear of any Running Line and within the Safety Points and Scotch Blocks; that the Points close properly; and that the Scotch Blocks are replaced across the rails after the operation is completed. Guards and Shunters are held responsible for seeing that the trains are clear of the Points, and that the Points are in proper position before a Signal is given to the Engine-drivers to move, and they must render the Signalmen every assistance they can in the shunting operations.

Vehicles to be placed within Safety Points and Scotch Blocks.

(*b*) In the case of a light engine unaccompanied by a Guard or Shunter, the Driver must satisfy himself that the Points are in the proper position.

186. (*a*) When vehicles are detached from a train and left on any Running Line prior to being shunted into Sidings, or when it is necessary for a train or any vehicle to be placed outside a

Vehicles left on any Running Line prior to being shunted.

Home Signal, the Signalman must be at once informed of the fact, in order that he may keep the Signals at Danger for the protection of the Line, and take the authorised steps for securing safety in one or both directions, as may be required. At night and in foggy weather or during falling snow, in addition, a Red Light must be shown at the rear of the vehicles, or, where necessary, at both front and rear, until they are safely placed in the Sidings. When vehicles have been detached care must be taken that they are properly secured so as to prevent their moving.

(*b*) During windy weather, or where the Line is not level, and a detached vehicle is likely to run away, the attention of the Signalman must be called to the fact of there being a vehicle to come off before it is detached.

(*c*) It is the duty of the shunter or person in charge of the Shunting to see that the necessary Red Light is shown at the rear, or, where necessary, at both front and rear, of vehicles standing on any Running Line, or on vehicles detached from trains, and Station-masters must take care that this is clearly understood by the men concerned. The Signalman must also keep a good look-out upon the arrival of trains, and if he see any vehicles have become detached and are left on any Running Line, he must take the necessary steps to protect them.

(*d*) Unless special permission is given, no train or vehicle must be placed outside a Home Signal where the Line is on a falling gradient towards the Signal-box in the rear.

187. (*a*) Vehicles must, when practicable, be attached to or detached from Passenger trains without the trains being moved.

Attaching and detaching to and from Passenger trains.

(*b*) Before any vehicle containing passengers is shunted over Points care must be taken to ascertain that the Points are securely set for the Line on which the vehicle is required to run, and that the Line is clear and properly protected.

(*c*) When vehicles are being moved by an engine for the purpose of being attached to a Passenger train, the Continuous Break pipes, where provided, must be connected, so that the break may be available during the operation.

188. (*a*) Before removing any Travelling Crane the person in charge of it must see that the jib is properly lowered and secured, and so fixed that it will pass under the gauge, and that the balance box is properly secured. When the Crane has to be conveyed by train it must, when practicable, be so placed that the jib points towards the rear of the train.

Removal of Travelling Cranes.

(*b*) Travelling Cranes must, when practicable, be forwarded only by Slow Goods Trains. The Station-master or person in charge, and the Head Guard of the train, must, before a Crane is attached to the train, take care that all the fastenings supplied for securing the jib and balance box, and, where provided, the side-stays of the truck, are in good condition and secured in their proper position, and that the necessary match or guard-waggons are provided. The Engine-driver must, before starting, be informed by the Head Guard that the Crane is being forwarded by the train, and at each stopping place on the journey the Guard must satisfy himself that the fastenings are secure. Waggon-examiners must also inspect the fastenings in addition to the usual examination of the wheels, &c. If any defect exists in any of the fastenings the Crane must not be attached to a train, and, if travelling, it must be detached for the fastenings to be made good.

Chains, &c., to be secured.

189. Foremen, Guards, and Shunters must take care that no timber-truck, boiler-waggon, or other vehicle provided with chains or other appliances is allowed to leave a Station or Siding without the chains and appliances being first carefully examined and made perfectly secure and safe, and Guards will be held responsible for seeing that they remain so during the journey.

Conveyance of articles of unusual length or weight.

190. (*a*) Long pieces of Iron, Round Timber, or other articles of unusual length, must not be despatched from Stations or Sidings, unless securely bound to the waggons with ropes, chains, or iron bands, care being taken that the loads are not too tightly bound to admit of the vehicles going easily round curves.

(*b*) Guards and Shunters must carefully examine loads of this description at places where the train may stop, to see whether they have shifted or require adjustment, and, if so, the waggons must not be taken on until the loads have been made secure.

(*c*) Furniture Vans, whether loaded or empty, must be secured by ropes in the waggons when conveyed by train.

(*d*) Special care must be exercised with loads of exceptional character as regards dimensions or weight, especially when sent from Private Sidings, to see that the loading is secure. The Locomotive, Engineering, and Waggon Departments must be consulted when necessary, and the loads inspected by an experienced person before being despatched.

(*e*) Waggons loaded with Engines, Anchors, Ships' Brackets, Boilers, Armour Plates, Long Timber, Steam Ploughs, Rails, exceptionally heavy machinery, or any other articles exceptionally heavy or lengthy, and Boiler or Oil Tank Waggons, whether empty or loaded, must not be conveyed by Express Goods trains.

Engine-driver or Guard to report any irregularity in working of Signals.

Cattle on Line.

Defects to be reported.

191. (*a*) Should an Engine-driver or Guard observe any irregularity in the working of Signals, or should he see any cattle or other obstruction on the Line, or any defect in the Signals, Works, Permanent-way, or Telegraph, he must report the same at the first Station at which the train stops, but if the circumstance be of a serious character he must stop the train at the first Signal-box, and give information.

Engine-driver to stop and give information.

(*b*) The Engine driver must, if necessary, also stop before reaching the Signal-box, to give information to Platelayers or other servants of the Company.

Engine-driver to signal train on opposite Line when necessary.

(*c*) The Engine-driver must also, if he see cattle on the Line, or observe anything wrong on the Line opposite to that on which his train is running, sound his whistle and exhibit a Danger Signal to any train he may meet; he must also, when practicable, place Detonators on the opposite Line of rails.

(*d*) At the end of his journey the Engine-driver must report the circumstance to his Superintendent, or Foreman, or Clerk in attendance, and the Guard must also report the case in his journal.

Train journals.

192. At the end of the journey the Guard in charge must deliver to the Station-master, or forward direct to the Superintendent, Goods Manager, or other Official as may be ordered, a journal containing the time of the running of his train, noting therein every circumstance of an unusual kind, any detentions that may have taken place on the journey, and any error as to parcels, luggage, or goods. In the event of any occurrence having taken place which might have involved, in any respect, the safety of the train or Line, he must, in addition to the notes in his journals, make a special report thereof.

Guard travelling in a train he is not appointed to work.

193. (*a*) When a Guard is riding in a train other than that he is appointed to work, he must, if so instructed, and his hours of duty will not be exceeded, render any assistance necessary in the working of the train by which he travels, and obey any instructions received from the Guard in charge of such train; and when there is on the train a break-van in which no Guard is riding, he must, when so instructed, ride in such van, and act as Assistant Guard.

(*b*) Passenger Guards, when waiting at Junction Stations, must assist with luggage, parcels, &c., to facilitate the despatch of the trains.

Change of Tail and Side Lamps.

194. (*a*) Should a vehicle be attached to, or detached from, the rear of a train at an intermediate Station, the Guard, if there be only one, or the Rear Guard if there be more than one, must see that the Tail and Side Lamps are in their proper places on the train.

(*b*) The Head Guard must see that the Continuous Break, Passenger Communications, and other couplings between the vehicles are properly adjusted after shunting is performed, and before again starting his train.

Continuous Break and other couplings to be adjusted after shunting.

195. Smoking in the carriages, except in the compartments specially set apart for that purpose, is strictly forbidden, and Guards must take care that the Bye-law on the subject is enforced. Guards must, before starting, see that they have a sufficient number of compartments reserved for smokers, and be careful not to place ladies in the compartments so reserved.

Smoking.

196. Should complaint be made of the running of any carriage, the Guard must report the fact to the Station-master or first Carriage-examiner, and enter the particulars in his journal, giving the number and class of carriage; but if the Guard have reason to apprehend danger from such carriage before it can be inspected, he must have it detached from the train.

Defective carriages.

197. When ladies are travelling alone the Guards must pay every attention to their comfort; and, in placing them in the train, they must, if requested, endeavour to select a compartment for them (according to the class of their tickets) in which other ladies are travelling. If ladies wish to change compartments during the journey the Guards must enable them to do so.

Ladies travelling alone.

Passenger changing into a superior class of carriage.

198. When a passenger is desirous of changing from an inferior to a superior class, the Guard must have this arranged by the Station-master or person in charge.

Carriage Racks.

199. The Racks in the carriages are provided for light articles only, and must not be used for boxes, portmanteaus, and other heavy articles of luggage, which must, if possible, be placed under the seats of the carriages when passengers desire to have the luggage with them, or otherwise loaded in the **Guards'** vans, or in the proper luggage compartments of the trains. Any infringement of this instruction is attended by risk of injury to passengers, and this must be explained to any passenger objecting to comply with it.

Parcels not to be thrown from trains.

200. Newspapers or other parcels must not be thrown from trains as they pass through intermediate Stations, unless specially sanctioned by the Superintendent of the Line. Where authority has been given for parcels to be thrown off, Guards must, before throwing the parcels from the train, satisfy themselves that the platforms are clear, and Station-masters and others must warn persons who may be about to keep clear of the train.

Deficiency or excess of room in train.

201. When a deficiency of room occurs in a train while on the journey, the Guard must request the Station-master to telegraph to the next Station where carriages are kept, to have one or more in readiness to attach on the arrival of the train, reporting the fact in his journal. He must also report in his journal if he has habitually either an excess or deficiency of room in his train.

202. The Guard must see that Platelayers and other workmen of the Company holding third-class passes are kept as separate as possible from the passengers. When a large number of workmen travel by the same train, carriages must be specially provided for their use, and they must ride in these carriages only.

Company's workmen to be kept apart from passengers.

203. Insane persons, and prisoners under the charge of police must not be placed with other passengers, but in a separate compartment.

Insane persons and prisoners.

204. In the event of any passenger being drunk or disorderly, to the annoyance of others, the Guard is to use all gentle means to stop the nuisance; failing which, he must, for the safety and convenience of all, have the offender removed from the train at the first Station. The Guard must obtain the name and address of the offender, and also of one, at least, of the passengers present at the time; he must also take care that the offender's luggage is put out of the train before it proceeds on its journey.

Disorderly Passengers.

205. (*a*) Guards, on arrival at a Ticket-collecting Station, must request the passengers to have their tickets ready, and must assist the Ticket-collectors by opening and closing the carriage doors; they must not, however, collect or examine tickets except under special instructions.

Collection or examination of tickets.

(*b*) Guards must also distinctly call out the names of the Stations at which the trains stop during the journey.

Calling out names of Stations.

206. (*a*) The Guard in charge of a Goods train must satisfy himself before starting, and during the journey, that the vehicles composing the train

Duties of Guard in charge of Goods train.

are properly loaded, marshalled, coupled, greased, and sheeted; that there are the prescribed number of breaks; that they are in good working order; that the train is in a state of efficiency for travelling; and that it has the proper Tail and Side Lamps attached to it. He must also carefully examine the loading of any vehicles he may attach on the way, and if any vehicle become unsafe from the shifting or derangement of the load, he must, at once, have the load re-adjusted or the vehicle removed from the train. All irregularities must be reported in his journals.

Doors of vehicles to be carefully examined.

(*b*) Before leaving Sidings and other places the doors of vehicles must be carefully examined to see that they are properly secured by the fastenings provided for the purpose.

Unsafe waggons not to travel.

(*c*) The Guard must not attach any waggon which he may think is unsafe to travel.

Guards not to attach waggons unless labelled on both sides.

(*d*) The Guard must not attach to his train any loaded waggon unless it is labelled or directed on both sides, nor any empty waggon which requires to be labelled or directed, unless such waggon is labelled or directed on both sides.

Loaded waggons to be labelled on both sides.

206A. (*a*) Every loaded waggon must be labelled or directed on both sides to its destination.

NOTE.—*This clause does not apply to Mineral traffic in train loads for journeys not involving marshalling during, or on completion of, the journey.*

Labelling of empty waggons.

(*b*) When it is necessary for any empty waggon to be labelled or directed to its destination, such waggon must be labelled or directed on both sides.

(*c*) Station-masters, Goods Agents, or other persons in charge will be held responsible for seeing that this regulation is complied with.

207. (*a*) Without the special authority of the Superintendent of the Line no Goods train must be run on any Running Line beyond the limits of Stations unless there is a break-van in the rear.

Break vans.

NOTE.—*For list of authorised exceptions see Appendix to Rule Book.*

(*b*) Where a train is authorised to run without a break-van in the rear, a break-van, or other suitable vehicle, for the use of the man in charge of such train, must be so attached as to be conveniently used by him, and also with due regard to safety in working the train. A Tail Signal must be carried on the last vehicle.

208. When it is necessary for any engine to run round a train, other than a Passenger train, between two Signal-boxes for the purpose of removing it from any Running Line, or when a train has to be removed by another engine attached to the rear, the train engine going forward, the train must first come to a stand at the Signal-box in the rear, when the Guard or Shunter must inform the Signalman what is about to be done. When the train is at a stand clear of the first Crossover-road the engine must be uncoupled, and a Lamp, showing a White Light by night or in foggy weather or during falling snow, must be placed by the Guard or Shunter on the leading end of the vehicle from which the engine has been detached. In the event of the vehicles being attached to the end of the train from which the engine has been uncoupled, the Lamp must be transferred to the

Engine running round a Goods train to remove it from Running Line.

front of the leading vehicle. The Lamp must remain on the vehicle until the train has been removed, to furnish evidence to the Signalman, when the train is drawn back, that it is complete.

Vehicles stopped for repairs.

209. (*a*) When a vehicle is not fit to travel it must be labelled by the Examiner with a Red "Not-to-Go" label, and must not be allowed to travel.

(*b*) When a vehicle requires repair, but is fit to travel, it must be labelled with a Green label, lettered "For Repairs," and be taken to the place indicated on the label.

(*c*) Any unauthorised person removing the label will render himself liable to criminal prosecution.

Doors of Live Stock waggons to be fastened.

Shunting of Live Stock

210. (*a*) When waggons of Live Stock are attached to a train the Guard must see that the fastenings of the doors are all secure. On the journey he must avoid unnecessarily shunting such waggons, and the shunting, when requisite, must be done as gently as possible.

Conveyance of Live Stock.

(*b*) Guards working trains by which Live Stock is conveyed must carefully examine the animals from time to time, as may be necessary, and satisfy themselves that they are travelling safely; if any are found down, or requiring attention, steps must be taken to have them put right as soon as possible, and a note of the circumstance must be made in the Guard's journal, the numbers of the waggons, and the sending and receiving Stations being also given.

(c) Loads of Live Stock received at Junctions from other Companies must be examined to see that they are in good condition when exchanged, and in case of injury or death, the attention of the other Company's servants must be drawn to the fact at the time.

Loads of Live Stock received at Junctions from other Companies.

211. When a Guard receives delivery at a Junction of home, foreign, or traders' Rolling Stock, in a damaged condition, he must draw the attention of the Clearing House Number-taker or the Station-master or person in charge to the circumstance, so that it may be noted. He must also note the circumstance in his journal.

Rolling Stock received damaged at Junctions, &c.

212. Guards must not take on waggons loaded with goods liable to be set on fire by sparks or hot cinders, unless the waggons are properly sheeted. Such waggons must be placed as far as possible from the engine.

Waggons loaded with goods liable to be set on fire.

213. Every Goods Guard who has used a van with a stove in it must, before leaving duty, take care that the fire in the stove is entirely extinguished, unless the van has to be sent out again immediately, in which case a small fire may be allowed to remain, all necessary precautions being taken to avoid damage arising therefrom.

Goods Guards' vans with stoves in them.

214. Goods Guards must not leave their trains until they have been delivered over to the Foreman, Yardman, Shunter, or Relief Guard.

Delivery of Goods train at end of journey.

215. Should a ballast train have to discharge or take up materials on any Running Line between two Signal-boxes, the Guard of such train must, before entering the Section, inform the Signalman in charge of the Signal-box of the fact, and of the probable time the work will

Ballast train discharging or taking up materials on Running Line between two Signal-boxes.

occupy, so that the Signalman may give any instructions that may be necessary as to the shunting of the ballast train for other trains.

Ballast train to be in charge of Guard.

216. (*a*) No ballast train must be allowed to run over the Line unless in charge of a Guard, who must have been passed as competent by the Traffic Department, and he will be responsible for the safe working of the train.

Guard to be accompanied by Flagman.

(*b*) The Guard must be accompanied by a Flagman, who must act under his instructions, and who must have been passed as competent by the Traffic or Engineer's Department, as the case may be.

NOTE.—*See explanation of this rule in Appendix to the Rule Book.*

TRAINS STOPPED BY ACCIDENT, FAILURE, OR OBSTRUCTION.

Protection of train.

217. (*a*) When a train is stopped by an accident or from any cause (unless it has arrived at or passed the Home Signal), the Guard, if there be only one, or the Rear Guard, if there be more than one, must immediately go back at least three-quarters of a mile, unless he arrive at a Signal-box within that distance, plainly exhibiting his Hand Danger Signal, to stop any following train, and, in addition to his Hand Signals, he must take Detonators (to be used by day as well as by night), which must be placed upon the Line on which the stoppage has happened as follows, viz. :—

1 Detonator a quarter of a mile from his train.

1 Detonator half a mile from his train, and

3 Detonators, ten yards apart, not less than three-quarters of a mile from his train;

and must also continue to exhibit his Hand Danger Signal to stop any coming train.

(*b*) If the Guard arrive at a Signal-box within or at about three-quarters of a mile from his train, he must place three Detonators on the Line opposite the Box, and must also instruct the Signalman to keep his Signals at Danger to protect the Line which is obstructed. He must then return to his train or take such other steps as may be necessary to deal with the obstruction.

(*c*) The Detonators must not be taken up until intimation has been received that the obstruction has been removed; and when the "Is Line Clear" Signal for the next train which has to pass through the Section has been accepted by the Signal-box in advance, the train must be stopped, and the Engine-driver must be advised of the circumstances, and instructed to travel cautiously through the Section.

(*d*) Should the distance of not less than three-quarters of a mile fall within a Tunnel, or close to the mouth of a Tunnel nearest to the obstruction, or in any other position where, owing to the formation of the Line, or to some other circumstance, the Engine-driver of an approaching train would be unable to obtain a good and distant view of the Hand Danger Signal, then, unless there be a Signal-box between the obstruction and the Tunnel, the Signal must be exhibited and Detonators must be placed on the Line at the end of the Tunnel farthest from the obstruction, or at such a distance over and above the prescribed distance of not less than three-quarters of a mile as may be necessary to ensure the Engine-driver obtaining a good and distant view of such Signal.

(*e*) Before the Guard in going back enters a Tunnel he must place three Detonators on the Line, ten yards apart, at the end of the Tunnel nearest to the obstruction.

(*f*) In order as quickly as possible to secure the safety of the Line as well as to obtain assistance and to regulate the working of the traffic, if the Signal-box in the rear of the obstruction be the nearer, the Guard, after protecting his train by Detonators, as directed above, must go to such Signal-box and advise the Signalman of the obstruction, but if the Signal-box in advance of the obstruction be the nearer or can be more quickly arrived at, the second Guard, if there be more than one Guard, or the Fireman, if there be not more than one Guard, must immediately go to the Signal-box and advise the Signalman of the cause of the obstruction.

(*g*) If the engine be able to run forward it must be detached, and the Driver must proceed to the Signal-box in advance for the purpose of carrying out the provisions of the previous paragraph, having, if required, first obtained from the Rear Guard an order to return on the wrong Line, as provided for in Rule 221.

When assistance is obtained from the rear.

(*h*) If the Guard obtain assistance from the rear he must ride on the engine of the assisting train, and point out to the Engine-driver the position of the disabled train. The assisting train must run at reduced speed, and great caution must be observed by all concerned.

(*i*) If the engine obtained from the rear has to return on the wrong Line the Guard must, before starting with the assisting engine, first obtain the prescribed "Wrong Line Order" in accordance with Rule 222.

(*j*) Except as above stated, the Guard must not return to his train until recalled by the Engine-driver sounding the whistle of his engine, and, when recalled, he must leave the three most distant Detonators, and return to his train, taking up the other Detonators on his way. Should he be recalled before reaching the prescribed distance, he must then place on the rail three Detonators, ten yards apart, and return to his train, taking up the other Detonators on his way.

Guard not to return to his train until recalled by Driver.

(*k*) Should the stoppage or failure occur to an engine not attached to a train, the Fireman must immediately go back and act in the way prescribed for the Guard.

When stoppage occurs to a light engine.

(*l*) Where Parallel Lines are so near together that a vehicle running on either Line fouls the other, Detonators must be placed on each Line.

Parallel Lines.

(*m*) When there are more than two Lines, and an accident causes more than one to be fouled, the necessary steps must be taken to protect all the Lines obstructed.

More than one Line obstructed.

218. (*a*) Should an accident to a train foul, or be dangerously near to, any Line used by trains running in the opposite direction, in addition to the Guard going back to protect the train in accordance with Rule 217, the Engine-driver of the disabled train must immediately detach his engine, if it be able to run forward, and proceed with it not less than three-quarters of a mile from the scene of accident, and there leave his Fireman with Detonators to act as laid down in Rule 217

When both Lines obstructed.

Fireman to protect opposite Line.

to protect the opposite Line; the Driver must then go forward with his engine to the nearest Signal-box and inform the Signalman of the obstruction, in order that any train running on the opposite Line may be stopped until the obstruction has been removed. In the course of the journey from the break-down to the Signal-box the Engine-driver must stop any train that may be approaching on the opposite Line by sounding his whistle, or the break-whistle where provided, exhibiting the necessary Hand Signals, and, in addition, showing a Red Head Light at night.

Engine disabled.

(*b*) Should the engine be disabled, or should there be any delay in detaching it, the Fireman must at once go forward and place the Detonators on the opposite Line, and also perform the duties of the Engine-driver as prescribed above.

Accident to engine, or train without Guard, and both Lines obstructed.

(*c*) Should an accident happen to an engine, or a train without a Guard, causing the obstruction of both Lines, the Engine-driver must immediately send his Fireman forward to stop trains travelling on the opposite Line, and must himself go back or send some other competent person, so that the obstruction may be protected in both directions.

Both Lines obstructed and Engine-driver not aware of accident.

219. (*a*) Should an accident to a train accompanied by only one Guard cause the obstruction of both Lines, and the Engine-driver run forward without being aware of the accident, the Guard must, if he can obtain the services of a competent person, send him forward to protect the opposite Line to that on which the train was running, and himself go back as directed in Rule 217.

(*b*) In the event of no competent person being at hand, the Guard must first go forward as quickly as possible, exhibiting his Hand Danger Signal, and place Detonators upon the opposite Line to that on which his train was running, as under, viz. :—

1 Detonator a quarter of a mile from the obstruction,
1 Detonator half a mile from the obstruction, and
3 Detonators, ten yards apart, not less than three-quarters of a mile from the obstruction ;

and then return and protect the rear of his train as prescribed in Rule 217.

Guard need not go prescribed distance if he arrive at a Signal-box.

(*c*) Should the Guard in going forward arrive at a Signal-box he need not go the prescribed distance, but must place three Detonators on the opposite Line at the Box, inform the Signalman of the circumstances, instruct him to keep the necessary Signals at Danger to protect the obstruction, and then return and protect the rear of his train as prescribed in Rule 217.

If Block System has failed.

(*d*) If the Block System has temporarily failed, the Guard must use his discretion as to which Line he protects first, having regard to all the circumstances, but he must use his best exertions to provide for the protection of both Lines with as little delay as possible.

Train divided.

220. The Engine-driver on seeing a Green Signal waved slowly from side to side from a Signal-box, must understand that his train is divided, and must exercise great caution by looking out for the second portion, and unless he has reason to believe the Line is not clear ahead, must not stop the portion attached to his engine until he is satisfied that the rear portion has been stopped, or is running very slowly. He must, however, observe and obey any Signals that may be exhibited against him.

Train or portion of train left on Running Line from accident or failure of engine.

221. (*a*) When a train or portion of a train is left on any Running Line from accident or inability of the engine to take the whole forward, or from any other cause, the Engine-driver must not return for it on the same Line, except as ordered in clauses (*f*) and (*g*) of this Rule, but must cross on to, and travel along, the proper Line, and must re-cross at the nearest point behind the part left, which he must push before him until convenient to go in front again with the engine. If there be a Crossover road immediately in front of the train, and the operation can be performed within sight of the Signalman, the Driver may use such Crossover road for the purpose of attaching his engine in front of the train.

Dividing Goods Trains.

(*b*) In cases where it is necessary to divide a Goods Train on an incline, owing to the inability of the engine to take the whole forward, both portions must, where practicable, be worked up the incline with a break-van in the rear. When a train is divided in this way at a Station, or at an intermediate Signal-box, where a portion of the train can be disposed of, it will generally be found most convenient to shunt the front portion of the train into a Siding, and take the rear portion forward first (with the break-van attached in rear) to the next Station or Signal-box where there are means of disposing of it.

After the first portion of the train has been disposed of, the engine must return on the proper line with the break-van, for the purpose of working forward the other portion of the train, which has been left behind, and the break-van must, in that case also, be attached in the rear.

Tail lamp.

(*c*) Unless both portions of the train are worked forward with a break-van in the rear, a Tail Lamp must not be carried on the engine or last vehicle of the front portion of the train before reaching the first Signal-box, where the Engine-driver must stop and inform the Signalman of the position of matters; if the engine or front portion of the train has to pass into the next Section a Tail Lamp must then be placed in the rear. The Signalman must not give "Train out of Section" to the Signal-box in the rear until he has satisfied himself that the whole of the train has arrived.

After sunset, or in foggy weather or during falling snow, before the front portion is drawn forward, a White Light must be exhibited on the front vehicle of the rear portion by the man who divides the train.

When two Guards with train.

(*d*) When two Guards are employed with the train the Front Guard (or where both Guards ride in the rear, the Under Guard) must uncouple it, and ride upon the last vehicle of the front portion; the other Guard, after putting on his break, and securing the last portion of the train so that it will remain stationary, must go back and protect it in accordance with Rule 217.

When only one Guard with train.

(*e*) When there is only one Guard with the train the Fireman must ride upon the last vehicle of the front portion, and the guard must take the necessary measures to protect the last portion.

Without a Crossover road.

When engine has to return on wrong Line to rear portion.

(*f*) If it be found necessary to return to the train or rear portion of the train on the wrong Line, the Engine-driver must, before starting with the front portion, send his Fireman to the Guard to obtain his written authority to the Signalman at the nearest Signal-box in advance where the front portion of the train can be put away, authorising him to allow the engine to return from that point on the wrong Line (see Form A at end of Rule), and without this authority the Signalman must not allow the engine to return on the wrong Line to its train. The Signalman must retain this Order. Should there, however, be an intermediate Signal-box, the Order held by the Engine-driver must be retained by him and shown to the Signalman there when running in the wrong direction, and given up to the Signalman at the place where the front portion of the train has been put away, when he arrives there with the second portion. After giving such instructions the Guard must continue to protect his train in the rear, and prevent a following train from pushing it ahead.

With a Crossover road.

If there is an intermediate Signal-box provided with a Crossover road between the point where the rear portion of the train is left on the Running Line and the Signal-box to which the front portion of the train will have to go to be disposed of, the "Wrong Line" order must be made out by the Guard to the Signalman at such intermediate Box, and the Driver, after leaving the order with the Signalman there, must proceed to the place where he can dispose of his train, and then return on the proper Line of rails to the intermediate Box, and be there crossed on to the line on which the rear portion of his train is standing, so that the engine shall not travel on the wrong Line further than is absolutely necessary.

Train standing on Running Line owing to failure of engine, or from any other cause.

(*g*) When a train is brought to a stand on any Running Line, owing to the failure of the engine, or from any other cause, and the Guard has gone to the rear to protect it, it may be necessary for the engine coming to the assistance of the train, or for the Breakdown Van train, to travel on the wrong Line from the Signal-box in advance. In such a case the Engine-driver of the disabled train must write out an authority (on Form B where in use, see end of Rule), for the Signalman at the Box in advance to allow the assistant engine, or the Breakdown Van train, to travel on the wrong Line to the disabled train. The Fireman of the disabled train must hand the written authority to the Signalman, and accompany the assistant engine, or the Breakdown Van train, to his train, advising the Engine-driver where, and under what circumstances, the disabled train is situated, and the Signalman must show the authority to the Driver before allowing the assistant engine or Breakdown Van train to proceed on the wrong Line. The Engine-driver of the disabled train, after giving the order for the assistant engine or the Breakdown Van train to run on the wrong Line, must not allow his train to be moved until the assistant engine or the Breakdown Van train arrives, unless satisfactory arrangements have been previously made to prevent the assistant engine or Breakdown Van train from coming on the wrong Line, and his Fireman has returned and handed the "Wrong Line" order back to the Engine-driver.

(*h*) Should there be any intermediate Signal-box without a Crossover road, the Fireman, when going for assistance, must show the written authority (on Form B where in use) to the Signalman at that Box.

Driver not to pass Signal box without Signalman's permission.

(*i*) The Engine-driver, when returning for the portion of his train that has been left behind, or when pushing such portion of his train, or the Driver of the assistant engine or the Break-down Van train, as the case may be, must not pass any Signal-box without the permission of the Signalman.

(*j*) If, after a train has become accidentally divided, both portions have been brought to a stand within sight of each other, and there is not a Signal-box near either end of the train, the front portion may be set back to the rear portion, provided the two portions can be re-coupled; but, before moving, the Engine-driver must send his Fireman to the Guard who is protecting the rear portion, for a written authority to set back.

To be printed on **Pink** *coloured paper.*

(*Front of Form A.*)

(**A supply of these Forms must be kept by each Guard.**)

To the Signalman at......... ..Signal-box.

Allow Driver of engine No...........to return on the wrong Line to the remainder of his train standing on the.............Line at .... I will prevent its being moved until the return of the engine.

Signed ....*Guard.*

Date...........190 Time issued......... m.

Catch Points exist at..............

(*Back of Form.*)

Here appears paragraph (*f*) of Rule 221.

To be printed on **Green** *coloured paper.*

(*Front of Form* B.)

(A supply of these Forms must be kept by each Engine-driver.)

To the Signalman at............Signal-box.

Allow an assistant engine or Break-down Van train to proceed on the wrong Line as authorised by Rule 221 (see other side) for my train which is stationary at ....I will not move my engine in any direction until the arrival of the assistant engine.

Signed....................*Driver.*

Date...........190 Time issued......... m.

Catch Points exist at...........

(*Back of Form.*)

Here appears paragraph (*g*) of Rule 221.

222. If, in case of accident, it is necessary for a train, or portion of a train, to return on the wrong Line to the Signal box in the rear, the Guard or Fireman must first go or send some other competent person to the Signalman there, and obtain his permission in writing for the train, or portion of train, to run on the wrong Line to his Box; but the Engine-driver must not move in the wrong direction until he has received such written permission (see Form C below).

Train, or portion of train, passing for short distance on wrong Line in case of accident.

To be printed on **Yellow** *coloured paper.*

(*Front of Form* C.)

(A supply of these Forms must be kept in each Signal-box.)

Authority for Engine-driver to travel on the wrong Line in case of Accident.

To Driver of engine No.........working......
......m. train
from...................to.......................

I authorise you to return with your train on the wrong Line to this Signal-box.

Signature of....................*Signalman*
at....................Signal-box.

Date...........190   Time issued...... m.

Catch Points exist at..............

(*Back of Form.*)

Here appears Rule 222.

When moving in wrong direction.

223. When moving in the wrong direction, as laid down in Rules 221 and 222, the Engine-driver must send his Fireman on foot in front of the engine to warn any one who may be on the Line that the engine or the Break-down Van train is approaching on the wrong Line. The Engine-driver must then proceed cautiously, travel at reduced speed, and make frequent use of the engine whistle.

224. Should Catch Points exist, arrangements must be made for securing them as shown in Rule 236, and Engine-drivers, when authorised to travel in the wrong direction under the circumstances referred to in Rules 221 and 222, must not pass over such Catch Points in the wrong direction until they have assured themselves that they are held or secured in their proper position for the train to run over them. Signalmen must, before authorising Engine-drivers to run in the wrong direction, remind them of the existence of the Catch Points.

Catch Points.

225. (*a*) In the event of any failure of, or accident to, some part of a train, it will generally be found desirable to bring the train to a stand as quickly as possible, but whether this course can be taken with safety, and how the stoppage can best be effected, must depend on the nature of the mishap to the train, the weight and speed of the train, the gradients, curves, and other conditions applying to the Line, particularly as regards the position of Points and Crossings. In all cases when the whole of the train remains upon the rails, it must be brought to a stand as quickly as possible.

Failure of, or accident to, some part of a train.

(*b*) If the engine be defective, the sooner the train can be stopped the better. If any of the vehicles be off the rails the breaks in the rear must be instantly applied, in order that by keeping the couplings tight the disabled vehicles may be kept up and out of the way of the vehicles behind

If engine defective.

until the force of the latter is exhausted, it being desirable that the front portion of the train should be brought slowly to a stand. The application of the front breaks might result in further damage, and great care must be exercised in their application. In all cases the application of breaks behind a disabled vehicle, or the application by the Guard of the Continuous Break at the rear of a train, will be attended with advantage, and Rear Guards of trains fitted with the Continuous Break must apply the Continuous Break as well as the Hand-break.

If Rear Guard does not promptly apply breaks.

(*c*) In the event of the Rear Guard not promptly applying the breaks when the Engine-driver whistles for them, the Engine-driver must, if his train is fitted with the Continuous Break, apply the same gradually, and with judgment and care.

If continuous break not in operation.

(*d*) Should any part of a train on which the Continuous Break is not in operation become detached when in motion, care must be taken not to stop the front part of the train before the rear portion has either been stopped or is running slowly, and the Rear Guard must promptly apply his break to prevent a collision with the front portion.

(*e*) In all cases Engine-drivers and Guards must act according to the best of their judgment and ability in the circumstances in which they are placed.

Train on fire.

226. Should any vehicle in a train be on fire the train must be stopped, and, if not protected by fixed Signals, the Guard must protect it in compliance with **Rule 217.** The Under Guard, or the Fireman if there be no Under Guard, must detach the vehicles in the rear of those on fire; the burning vehicles must be drawn forward to a distance of fifty yards at least, then uncoupled, and left properly secured, until the fire can be extinguished, to effect which every effort must be made.

WORKING TRAFFIC OF A DOUBLE LINE, OVER A SINGLE LINE OF RAILS DURING, REPAIRS OR OBSTRUCTION.

227. (*a*) When it is necessary, during repairs or owing to an obstruction of any kind, to work the traffic in both directions over a Single Line, the following precautions must be adopted :—

When any obstruction.

(i) A competent person must be appointed as Pilotman, who must wear round his left arm, above the elbow, a distinctive Badge (see end of Rule). Until the regular Badge can be obtained the Pilotman must wear a Red Flag tied round his left arm. No engine must enter upon any portion of the Single Line without the Pilotman being PRESENT and riding upon the said engine, unless two or more trains are required to follow in the same direction, in which case the Pilotman must order all trains to proceed except the last, upon the engine of which he must ride. In the case of an engine assisting in the rear of the last train, the Pilotman must ride on the assisting engine. If a special engine is supplied for the

Appointment of Pilotman.

Pilotman's Badge.

Pilotman to be present.

use of the Pilotman he must, after personally starting the whole of the trains, follow or accompany the last train. When it is necessary for the Pilotman's engine to accompany the last train it must be attached to the front of that train, but the Pilotman must ride on the train-engine.

(ii) The Pilotman must show himself to the Signalman at each Box he passes.

Additional precautions.

(*b*) In addition to the foregoing precautions, three Detonators must be placed at both ends of the Line obstructed, a quarter of a mile from the point where Single Line Working commences, and a Red Flag by day, and a Red Light by night, or in foggy weather or during falling snow, must also be placed on the blocked Line near to the Detonators.

The Detonators must be placed on each side of the obstruction as shown in the following diagram. When the distance from the obstruction to the Crossover road is less than a quarter of a mile, the Detonators must be placed as far from the obstruction as circumstances permit. A Hand-signalman must also be placed outside the Distant

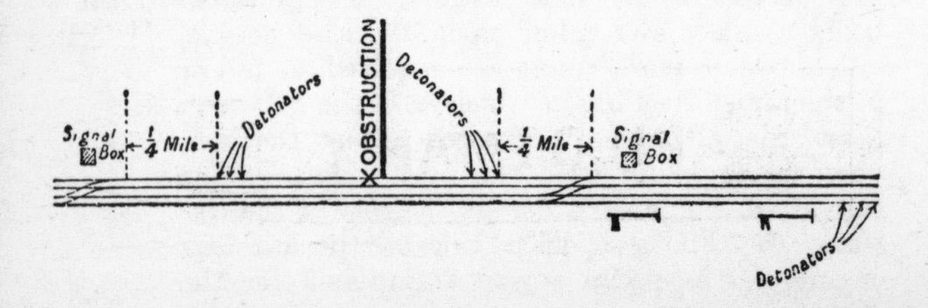

Signal applicable to the Line upon which Single Line Working is in operation, and he must place three Detonators on the rail for each approaching train.

(c) If the obstruction has been caused by a disabled train or engine, no portion of the train or the disabled engine must be allowed to foul the Crossover road at either end of the Single Line Working unless the Pilotman is present.

(d) Before Single Line Working is put in operation, the Signalman at each end of the Single Line must, when practicable, advise the Signalman at the Box in the rear, and the latter must stop each train proceeding in the direction of the Single Line Working, inform the Engine-driver of the circumstances, and instruct him to proceed cautiously, the trains being accepted by the Signalmen at each end of the Single Line in accordance with clause 5 of the Block Telegraph Regulations.

NOTE.—*The distinctive Badge must be a Red Armlet with the word "Pilotman" shown thereon in white letters, thus:—*

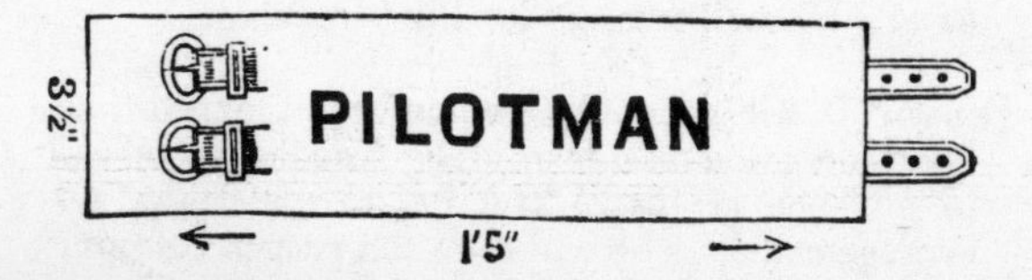

Limit of Single Line Working.

When Cross-over road, where there are no Fixed Signals, is used.

When Hand Signal at ¾ mile cannot be plainly seen by Engine-driver.

228. Single Line Working should be confined to points at which there are Fixed Signals with a Crossover road, and at all times to the shortest length possible; but in the event of a Crossover road not protected by Fixed Signals being used for Single Line Working, a competent man, with the necessary Signals, must be placed at least three-quarters of a mile beyond the Crossover road to signal in place of the Distant Signal, and another man (similarly provided) at the Points to signal in place of the Home Signal. Should the distance of three-quarters of a mile fall within a Tunnel, or close to the mouth of a Tunnel nearest to the obstruction, or in any other position where, owing to the formation of the Line, or to some other circumstance, the Engine-driver of an approaching train would be unable to obtain a good and distant view of the Signal, then the Signal must be exhibited at the end of the Tunnel farthest from the Crossover road, or at such a distance over and above the prescribed distance of three-quarters of a mile as may be necessary to ensure the Engine-driver obtaining a good and distant view of such Signal.

Arrangements for Pilot-working.

229. (*a*) If the speaking Telegraph or Telephone communication is available, the Station-masters or other responsible officials at both ends of the obstructed Section must communicate with each other by telegraph or telephone, and agree as to who shall arrange for Pilot-working.

(*b*) It will generally be found most expeditious for the Station-master or other responsible official in advance of the obstruction to undertake the arrangements, as he will have the proper Running Line clear on which the Pilotman with the Forms can make his first journey by train or lorry if either is available. Under no circumstances must a train or lorry be allowed to run over the Single Line *in the wrong direction* until the Pilotman holds upon his Form the signatures of the Signalman at each end of the Single Line Section, and also at any intermediate Signal-box.

Forms to be used.

(*c*) A sufficient number of the Forms (see pages 137 and 138 for specimen Form) provided for the purpose of establishing Single Line Working must be filled up and signed by the Station-master or person arranging the Single Line Working. One of these, signed by the Pilotman, he must deliver, in the presence of the Pilotman, to the Signalman in charge of the Crossover road at which the Single Line Working commences; one signed by the Signalman must be handed to the Pilotman, who must also sign it, and the remainder must be conveyed by the Pilotman to the other end of the Section which has to be worked as a Single Line. On his way the Pilotman must verbally inform the persons in charge of Level Crossings, Platelayers, and any other men at work on the Line, that Single Line Working is about to be commenced and which Line will be used; he must also leave a copy of the Form (signed by himself) with the person in charge of any intermediate Signal-box or Station then open between the points between which Single Line Working is about to be put into operation, and each of such persons must sign the Form held by the Pilotman. On his arrival at the other end of the Single Line Section the Pilotman must deliver a copy (signed by himself) to the Station-master or person in charge, and another (also signed by himself) to the Signalman on duty, each of whom must also sign the Form held by the Pilotman. Trains may then be allowed to pass to and fro on the Single Line by the permission and under the control of the Pilotman.

(*d*) When a Station-master himself acts as Pilotman he must also address and give a copy of the Form to the person he leaves in charge of his Station.

(*e*) Should any intermediate Signal-box or Station be opened after Single Line Working has been commenced, the Pilotman must, as soon as practicable, advise the person in charge of such Signal-box or Station that Single Line Working is in operation, and obtain his signature on the Form in the usual way. He must also hand to the Signalman or Station-master a copy of the Single Line Working Form.

Telegraph or telephone messages.

(*f*) All telegraph or telephone messages sent or received in connection with the arrangements for working Single Line must be written on the usual message forms, and telephone messages must be repeated back by the receiving Station, copies of the messages being afterwards forwarded to the Superintendent.

Suspension of Block Telegraph Working.

230. (*a*) When Single Line has to be worked, and it is necessary to suspend Block Telegraph Working, this must be done only by the person who arranges the Single Line Working, by an order in writing on the Single Line Working Form, but in foggy weather or during falling snow, or when a Tunnel intervenes, or the gradients are heavy on the Section of the Line where the traffic has to be worked on a Single

In foggy weather or during falling snow, or where Tunnel

Line, Block Telegraph Working must be maintained on such Section, the Up trains being signalled on the Up Line Block Telegraph Circuit, and the Down trains on the Down Line Block Telegraph Circuit, or the Pilotman must accompany every train passing over the Single Line.

intervenes, or gradients heavy, Block Telegraph Working to be maintained.

(*b*) When Block Telegraph Working has to be maintained, and the Block Indicator is at the "Train on Line" position for the train which has caused the obstruction, the Signalman at the Box in advance of the obstruction must, in order that the Block Signalling of trains in both directions on the Single Line may be carried on as laid down in the foregoing paragraph, liberate the Block Indicator in accordance with the following instructions:—

Block Indicator to be liberated.

(i.) When the Station-master in advance of the obstruction arranges Single Line Working, and the necessary Form has been conveyed to the Signalman in the rear, the Signalman in the rear must, provided the train, if the Pilotman has been conveyed by train, has arrived complete, give the "Train out of Section" Signal, and the Signalman in advance of the obstruction, after acknowledging such Signal, must release the Block Indicator for the Line which is obstructed.

(ii.) If the Pilotman is not conveyed through the Section by train, he must, when the arrangements for commencing working Single Line have been completed, instruct the Signalman at the Box in the rear of the obstruction to so inform the Signalman at the Box in advance; the latter Signalman must then release the Block Indicator for the obstructed Line.

(iii.) When the Station-master in the rear of the obstruction arranges Single Line Working, and the necessary Form is conveyed to the Signalman in advance of the obstruction, the Pilotman, when handing the Signalman the Form, must request him to release the Block Indicator for the train which caused the obstruction.

NOTE.—*Clause (b) is not applicable to Lines worked on the Lock and Block System or with Block Indicators showing two positions only.*

Engine-driver and Guard or Guards of train about to enter upon Single Line to be informed that Single Line is being worked.

231. (*a*) No train must be allowed to enter upon the Single Line without the Engine-driver and Guard or Guards having first been informed by the Pilotman that Single Line is being worked, and the points between which it is in operation.

Two or more trains following.

(*b*) When two or more trains are allowed to follow in the same direction, and Block Telegraph Working is suspended, the Engine-driver of each following train must be told by the Pilotman what interval of time has elapsed since the preceding train left.

Signalmen to know Pilotman.

232. (*a*) The Signalman at each end of the Single Line must know the man appointed as Pilotman, and must keep at Danger the Signals applicable to trains entering upon the Single

Line until both Lines are safe, and the ordinary working of the traffic is resumed; but Engine-drivers may pass the Signals at Danger when so instructed by the Pilotman.

Signals applicable to trains entering upon Single Line.

(*b*) When Block working is maintained, the fixed Signals at intermediate Boxes must (except where the Lock and Block system of train signalling is in operation) be worked for trains passing over the Single line in both directions. Where the Lock and Block system is in force or when Block working is suspended, the fixed Signals must be kept at Danger, and the Signalman must Hand-signal the Engine-driver past the Signals when the line is clear for the train to proceed.

Working of Signals at intermediate Boxes.

(*c*) When Block Telegraph Working is maintained the Pilotman must obtain the permission of the Signalman before allowing a train to enter upon the Single Line.

Pilotman to obtain Signalman's permission before allowing train to enter Single Line.

233. (*a*) When both Lines are blocked and it becomes necessary to work trains up to the obstruction on both sides, for the transfer of passengers or any other purpose, Single Line Working must be arranged on both sides, between the nearest Crossover road and the obstruction, a Pilotman being appointed to act on each side in accordance with these Regulations.

Transfer of passengers when both Lines are blocked.

(*b*) Two competent men, provided with the necessary Hand Signals and Detonators, must be appointed to protect the obstruction, one on each side.

Obstruction to be protected.

(*c*) After making the necessary arrangements for the safety of the passengers and trains, it will

Forwarding of passengers.

be the duty of the Guards and Engine drivers (if no superior officer be present) to arrange for the passengers being forwarded as soon as possible, acting in strict accordance with these Regulations.

When one Line is cleared.

(*d*) When one Line is cleared arrangements must be made for Single Line Working between the Crossover roads on each side of the obstruction. Both Pilotmen must proceed with the first train over the Line which has been cleared, and the person who is appointed Pilotman for that Line must withdraw all the Single Line Forms previously in use, at the same time that he delivers the new Forms.

Speed of trains.

234. Trains when working over the Single Line must be run cautiously and at reduced speed, and Engine-drivers must make frequent use of the Engine-whistle. When passing through a Tunnel, or after sunset or in foggy weather or during falling snow, they must carry a Red Head Light.

Points which become Facing Points to be held or secured.

235. All Points, which become Facing Points to trains running over the Single Line, must either be held by a competent man appointed to the duty, or so secured as to enable the trains to pass safely over them.

Catch Points.

236. (*a*) Where there are Catch Points, Station-masters, Signalmen, and others must take care, before Single Line Working is put in operation over such Catch Points, that a man, provided with proper Signals, is placed at them, with special orders to remain there, and to hold them properly closed or see that they are firmly secured for the safe passage of each facing train, until the order for Single Line Working has been withdrawn, and Double Line Working resumed.

(*b*) When a train is approaching Catch Points in the facing direction, the man at the Points must, when they are right for the train to pass over them, give the Engine-driver a Green All Right Signal held steadily in the hand.

(*c*) The Pilotman must satisfy himself that the Engine-driver is aware of the position of the Catch Points.

Engine-driver to satisfy himself that Catch Points are in proper position.

237. Engine-drivers must not when working Single Line, as above, pass any Catch Points in the facing direction until they have assured themselves that they are in the proper position for their trains to run over; nor, where a man is employed at the Catch Points, until they have received a Signal to do so from the man at the Points.

Change of Pilotman.

238. (*a*) Should the Pilotman give up the working to another, fresh Forms must be issued on which the name of the new Pilotman must be inserted. The fresh Forms must be delivered by the new Pilotman and substituted for the old Forms, and the necessary signatures obtained on the fresh Forms. He must at the same time withdraw the old Forms.

The issue of the new Forms must only be done by the person who arranged the Single Line Working, to whom the new Pilotman must afterwards deliver the old Forms.

(*b*) After one Pilotman has been relieved by another, the Pilotman who has been relieved must not ride upon any engine until he resumes duty as Pilotman.

Signalmen changing duty.

(*c*) Should the Signalmen be changed during the time Single Line Working is in operation, the man coming on duty must be made acquainted, by the man going off duty, with the arrangement in force and with the person acting as Pilotman, and he must, before taking charge of the Signal-box, countersign the form held by the Pilotman.

Resumption of Double Line Working.

239. (*a*) When the Line is clear all the Forms issued for the Single Line Working must be collected by the Pilotman, and afterwards sent to the Superintendent.

For the purpose of collecting the Forms the Pilotman may use, in the proper direction, the Line which had been obstructed. He must, however, before taking a train over that Line, have a clear understanding with all concerned.

Pilotman to accompany first train passing over Line.

(*b*) The Pilotman must accompany the first train passing over the Line on which the obstruction existed.

(*Form referred to in Rule* 229.)

Great Western Railway.

SINGLE LINE WORKING DURING REPAIRS OR OBSTRUCTION.

This Form must be filled up and used whenever it is temporarily necessary to work the traffic of a Double Line over a Single Line.

..................................*Station.*

...................................190

The.............Line being blocked between ....and......................, all Traffic will pass between those two places on the.......................Line.

........................will act as Pilotman, and no train must be allowed to pass on to the Single Line unless he is present, and personally orders the train to start.

Block Telegraph Working must be......... *Insert "Maintained" or "Suspended," as the case may be.*

This Order is to remain in force until withdrawn by the Pilotman.

Catch Points exist at........., and arrangements have been made for working as directed in Rule 236.

If no Catch Points exist, erase this clause.

(Signed)..........................

To.....................

[*Continued.*

	TIME.
*Noted by....................at.........	....
*Noted by....................at.........	....
*Noted by....................at.........	....
*Noted by....................at.........	....
*Noted by....................at.........	....
*Noted by....................at.........	....
Noted by.........................Pilotman.	

* *These signatures must only be made on the copy held by the Pilotman.*

Twelve of these Forms must be kept in a convenient place at each Station, and at every Signal-box where there is a Crossover road, so as to be available at any moment, night or day.

Before Single Line Working is commenced a copy of this Form must be signed by the Signalman and person in charge at each end of the Single Line, and at each intermediate Signal-box or Station, and be kept by the Pilotman, who must see that each of the men signing the Form retains a copy for himself.

In the event of a Station-master himself acting as Pilotman, he must address and give a copy of the Form to the person he leaves in charge of his Station.

Station-masters and persons in charge receiving this Form will be held responsible that the Inspectors, Foremen, Signalmen, and others concerned at their Station are immediately made acquainted with the circumstances, and are instructed in their necessary duties.

PERMANENT-WAY AND WORKS.

Men in charge to be provided with Regulations and Working Time-table.

240. There must be a Foreman, Ganger, or Leading Man for each Gang of Platelayers or men engaged on the Permanent-way or on other Works affecting the Running Lines, and the District Inspector of Permanent-way must take care that every such Foreman, Ganger, or Leading Man under his control, is provided with a copy of the current Working Time-table, the Appendix thereto, where issued, and the Weekly and any other Notices of the Working arrangements, and that each Foreman, Ganger, Leading Man, and Under Man is provided with a copy of these Rules and Regulations.

Men to be provided with copy of Rules.

241. Each Foreman, Ganger, or Leading Man, and every man engaged on the Permanent-way or Works affecting the Running Lines, must constantly have with him when on duty a copy of these Rules and Regulations, which he must produce when required. The Foreman, Ganger, or Leading man in charge must read and explain, or cause to be read and explained, the Rules and Regulations, so far as they relate to his duties, to every man who is employed in his Gang, both at the time he first comes to work under him and at least twice a year afterwards. Each man to whom the Rules and Regulations are so read and explained must sign a declaration to that effect, which must be sent to the Permanent-way Inspector of the district.

Rules to be read and explained to men.

242. The Inspectors of Permanent-way and Works must take care that all Rules and Regulations are observed, and report any departure from them to the Engineer.

Observance of Rules.

243. Each Inspector must have a register of the names and places of residence of all the men employed in his district, so that in case of accident he may be enabled to summon them immediately to assist in any way that may be required. Should any obstruction take place, caused by snow, frost, slips, or other sudden emergency, he must immediately collect the number of men required.

Inspectors to have register of names and addresses of men.

To summon men in emergency.

244. (*a*) Each Gang of Platelayers or Labourers must be supplied by the Inspector of Permanent-way for the district with two Red and two Green

Lamps and Signals to be supplied.

Flags, two Hand Signal Lamps, and a proper number of Detonators. Each Ganger will be held responsible for having his Signals constantly in proper order and ready for use. The Flags must be used during daylight, the Lamps after sunset and in foggy weather or during falling snow, and the Detonators whenever necessary to attract the attention of Engine-drivers.

Meaning of Signals.

(*b*) The Red Signal indicates Danger, and must be used only when it is necessary to stop a train.

(*c*) The Green Signal waved slowly from side to side by Platelayers indicates that trains must reduce speed to fifteen miles an hour or such other speed as may be prescribed over the portion of Line protected by such Green Signal.

When speed has to be reduced where vehicles are slipped.

(*d*) If it become necessary that the speed of trains should be thus reduced when approaching a Station where it is appointed for vehicles to be slipped, the Foreman Platelayer or Ganger must advise the Station-master at such Station, and, until the speed restriction can be withdrawn, the Station-master must, unless instructions are issued to the contrary, arrange for the Fixed Signals to be kept at Danger to stop the trains which ordinarily slip vehicles at his Station; he must also, if time permit, advise the Station-master at the last stopping Station that the train must be stopped instead of the carriages being slipped.

Fixed Signals not to be used except in cases of emergency.

245. Platelayers and Labourers must not, except in cases of emergency, or as provided in Rules 249, 250, 251, 253, and 254, avail themselves of the Fixed Signals, but must, in all cases, use their own Signals for their own purposes.

246. A lorry must not be placed on the Line, except by the Platelayers, and with the knowledge of the Ganger, who is responsible for seeing it properly used and protected. It must not be attached to a train, and when not in use must be taken off the rails, placed well clear of the Line, and the wheels secured with chain and padlock.

Lorries to be placed on Line by Platelayers only. Lorry not to be attached to train, and to be left clear of Line.

247. Before leaving or passing any Station or other place where there are Fixed Signals, or fouling any Junction, the Foreman or Ganger in charge of a lorry must advise the Signalman on duty of the destination of the lorry, and of the work it is going to do, and must not proceed until he has obtained the Signalman's permission.

Signalman to be advised of destination of lorry, and work it is going to do.

248. (*a*) When a lorry is run empty or used for conveying materials or men along the Line, it must be taken in the same direction as the trains run, and followed at a distance of not less than three-quarters of a mile by a man with Hand Danger Signals and Detonators. On a Single Line, the lorry must be protected in both directions, except when the lorry is used for conveying the Pilotman through the Section owing to the failure of the Electric Train Tablet or Train Staff apparatus (see Rule 25 of Electric Staff and Tablet Instructions, and Rule 14 of the Train Staff and Ticket Instructions in the Appendix), in which case it will not be necessary to protect it in either direction.

Protection of lorry on Running Line.

(*b*) A lorry must not be run in the wrong direction on any Running Line.

Lorry not to be run in wrong direction.

249. (*a*) When it is necessary for a Platelayers' lorry to go through any of the Tunnels specially enumerated in the Appendix to the

Lorries going into or through Tunnels.

Working Time-table as coming within the application of this Rule, it will be signalled on the Block Instruments in accordance with the authorised Code, and the Signalman at the Box in advance will, if the Line be clear to the Home Signal, give permission for the lorry to approach his Box. No train will be allowed to enter the Tunnel on the same Line until the "Train out of Section" Signal has been received from the Signal-box in advance, to indicate that the lorry has left the Tunnel and has passed the next Block Signal-box or been taken off the rails. Should the lorry, after passing through the Tunnel, be removed from the rails before reaching the next Signal-box, the Ganger must go forward and inform the Signalman that the lorry is clear of the Line.

(*b*) If, however, time would be saved, the Ganger must return to the Signal-box in the rear, and inform the Signalman that the lorry is clear of the Line; the Signalman will then send the "Cancelling" Signal to the Signal-box in advance.

(*c*) Lorries passing through all other Tunnels must be protected solely by the Platelayers' own Signals.

(*d*) Where the Line is worked on the Electric Train Tablet or Electric Train Staff Block system the Ganger or Leading Man in charge of the lorry must be in possession of the Tablet or Staff. Should the lorry, after passing through the Tunnel, be removed from the rails before reaching the next Tablet or Staff Station, the Ganger or Leading Man must take the Tablet or Staff to the Signalman at the end of the Section nearest to him (except when the Tablet cannot be restored to the instrument from which it was obtained, in which case it must be taken to the Tablet Station at the opposite end of the Section), and he must inform the Signalman that the lorry is clear of the Line and hand the Tablet or Staff to him.

250. (*a*) Before any truck, lorry, waggon, or other obstruction is placed upon the Line, or in the event of any Ballast or other Way and Works train being obliged to remain stationary on the Line, or to move so slowly as to be in danger of being overtaken, the Danger Signal must be plainly exhibited, and three Detonators placed upon the Line, ten yards apart, at a distance of not less than three-quarters of a mile from the obstruction, in the direction of any coming train (even if no train is expected), by the Foreman or Ganger, or by a competent man appointed by him to do the duty, who must continue to exhibit the Signal and keep the Detonators on the Line until he receives an order from the Foreman or Ganger to withdraw the Signal; such order, however, must not be given until the obstruction is completely removed.

Protection of Running Line in case of obstruction.

(*b*) If the obstruction occur on a Single Line of Railway, the Foreman or Ganger must arrange for the Danger Signals to be exhibited and three Detonators placed on the Line, ten yards apart, not less than three-quarters of a mile in both directions, unless the obstruction is caused by a Ballast train in possession of a Train Staff or Tablet when it will not be necessary to send out a Flagman to protect it.

Obstruction of Single Line.

NOTE.—*For modification of this R le on certain Single Lines see Appendix to Rule Book.*

Obstruction near a Tunnel.

(*c*) Should the distance of not less than three quarters of a mile fall within a Tunnel, or close to the mouth of a Tunnel nearest to the obstruction, or in any other position where, owing to the formation of the Line or to some other circumstance, the Engine-driver of an approaching train would be unable to obtain a good and distant view of the Hand Danger Signal, then the Signal must be exhibited and Detonators must be placed on the Line at the end of the Tunnel farthest from the obstruction, or at such a distance over and above the prescribed distance of not less than three-quarters of a mile as may be necessary to ensure the Engine-driver obtaining a good and distant view of such Signal.

(*d*) Before the person in going back enters the Tunnel, he must place three Detonators on the Line, ten yards apart, at the end of the Tunnel nearest to the obstruction.

Flagman.

(*e*) If the person appointed to exhibit the necessary Signals and to place the Detonators on the Line, should arrive at a Signal-box before he has reached the prescribed distance, he must request the Signalman in charge of it to keep his Signals at Danger to protect the Line about to be obstructed, and, except as provided in the following paragraph, it will not be necessary for him to go further back, but he must remain at the Signal-box, put down three Detonators, and use his Hand Danger Signals; and the Signalman so instructed must not take off his Signals or allow any train to pass his Box in the direction of the obstruction until the Flagman, or Foreman, or Ganger in charge of the work has informed him that the obstruction has been removed, and that the Line is clear and safe for the passage of trains;

the object being that the Signalman and Platelayers shall not show contrary Signals to approaching Engine-drivers.

(*f*) If the obstruction is less than a quarter of a mile in advance of the Home Signal applicable to the Line which is obstructed, the Flagman must not remain at such Signal-box, but after instructing the Signalman to keep his Signals at Danger for the protection of the obstruction must go back the required distance of three-quarters of a mile, as ordered in the first paragraph of this Rule, unless there is another Signal-box within that distance, when he must stop at such Box, and act as above directed.

251. (*a*) Before a rail is taken out, or relaying operations are commenced, or in case of any slip or failure of the works, or if from any cause the Line is unsafe, a Flagman appointed for the purpose must go back, exhibiting a Danger Signal, and place three Detonators on the Line, ten yards apart, at a distance of not less than one mile from the obstruction; in the case of a Single Line, or where the slip or failure affects both Up and Down Lines, this must be done in both directions.

Signals during relaying, &c.

NOTE.—*For modification of this Rule on certain Single Lines see Appendix to Rule Book.*

(*b*) The Flagman in going out to perform the duty must act in accordance with Rule 250.

Flagman.

(*c*) Before a rail is taken out, the Platelayers must have, at the spot, a perfect rail in readiness to replace it.

Changing Rail.

252. (*a*) In addition to sending out a Flagman the prescribed distance, as directed in Rules 250

Additional Flagmen.

and 251, the Foreman or Ganger must also station near to the working party a second Flagman, who must place two Detonators on the rail, ten yards apart, and exhibit a Danger Signal

(*b*) When the distant Flagman is out of the sight of the Flagman stationed near to the working party, one or more Flagmen, as may be necessary, must be stationed intermediately, for the purpose of repeating to the distant Flagman the Signals exhibited by the home Flagman.

Signals when repairing Line.

253. (*a*) When repairing, lifting, or slewing the Line, or when performing any other operation, or during any other time when it is necessary for a train to travel at reduced speed, the Foreman or Ganger must send a man back at least half a mile, or as much further as the circumstances of the case render necessary, who must fix a Detonator on one rail of the Line for which he is signalling, and exhibit a Caution Signal, by waving a Green Flag or a Green Light slowly from side to side, so as to be plainly visible to the Engine-driver of an approaching train.

(*b*) The same precautions must be adopted by night as well as by day when it is necessary for trains to travel at reduced speed.

(*c*) If the man in going back should arrive at a Signal-box, or if the work is near to a Signal-box and within the protection of the Home Signal of such Box, he need not proceed beyond the Box, but he must advise the Signalman in charge of it of the necessity for slackening the speed of any train running in the direction of the repairs, and, when the Fixed Signals are lowered, he must himself exhibit the Caution Signal by waving a Green Flag or a Green Light slowly from side to side, so as to be plainly visible to the Engine-driver of the approaching train, but he need not place a Detonator on the rail unless it is necessary to do so to attract the attention of the Engine-driver as directed in Rule 244.

(*d*) In such cases the Signalman must keep his Danger Signals exhibited until the speed of the train has been sufficiently reduced, when he must, if the Block Telegraph or other Regulations have been complied with, lower his Signals to allow the train to pass.

(*e*) Where the necessity for trains to travel at reduced speed continues for a lengthened period, the Engineer may dispense with the placing of Detonators on the rail, and also the exhibition of the Hand Caution Signal; in substitution thereof, a Warning Board painted green, and of the following shape, must be fixed not less than half a mile from the place to be protected, and in such a position as to be clearly seen by Engine-drivers. During the night one Green and one White Light must be placed side by side on the Warning Board, thus:—

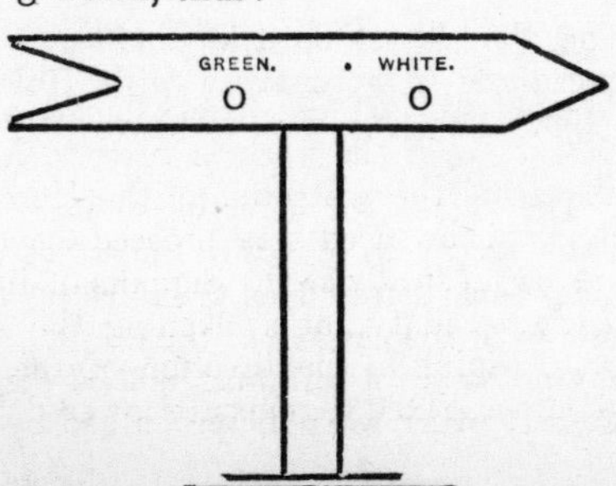

(*f*) Warning Boards must only be brought into use after due notice has been given in the weekly or other Notices indicating the positions of the Boards and the places to which they refer.

(*g*) The precise position of the work or place for which the Warning Board is intended will be indicated by a flagman on the ground, and Engine-drivers must keep a good look-out for this man and obey any Signals given by him.

(*h*) In foggy weather or during falling snow a Flagman must be sent back, and he must act as prescribed in clause (*a*) hereof.

Obstruction of Line between Up and Down Distant Signals.

254. (*a*) When it is necessary to obstruct the Line, as described in Rules 250, 251, and 253, between the Up and Down Distant Signals of any Station, Junction, or intermediate Signal-box, the permission of the Signalman must be first obtained by the Foreman or Ganger, and the Fixed Signals applicable to the Line about to be obstructed must not, except as provided in Rule 253, be lowered for a train to pass until the Signalman has been informed by the same Foreman or Ganger that the Line is again clear and safe for the passage of trains.

(*b*) The Platelayers must, in addition, protect their operations in accordance with Rules 250, 251, or 253.

Times for effecting repairs.

Rails not to be displaced in foggy or snowy weather, except absolutely necessary.

255. The times for effecting repairs which involve the stopping of trains must, as far as practicable, be so selected as to interfere as little as possible with the passage of the traffic. Unless absolutely necessary a rail must not be displaced, nor must any other work be performed by which an obstruction may be caused to the passage of the trains in a fog or during falling snow.

256. Persons in charge of Ballast trains must obey the orders of the Station-masters, Inspectors, and Signalmen, so far as relates to the time of their running on the Line.

Persons in charge of Ballast trains to obey orders of Station-masters, Inspectors, and Signalmen.

257. Ballast trains and men employed with such trains and all extra gangs must not work on the Running Lines during a fog or falling snow, except when authorised under special circumstances, and no Ballast train, waggon, truck, or lorry must be used, if possible to avoid it, except during daylight and when the weather is sufficiently clear for a Signal to be distinctly seen at a distance of half a mile.

Ballast trains and men not to work on Running Lines during fog or falling snow.

No Ballast train to be run, or lorry used, except during daylight.

258. (*a*) Any accident to a train, or failure of any part of the Works affecting the safety of the Line, must be reported as soon as possible to the nearest Inspector of Permanent-way and to the Station-masters on both sides of the point at which the accident or failure has occurred; and, in the event of a Signal-box intervening between the point of accident or failure and the nearest Station in either direction, the occurrence must also be reported to the Signalman on duty.

Accident to train, or failure of Works to be reported.

(*b*) To convey intelligence of, or to summon assistance to, any accident or failure, a Platelayer must be sent, as quickly as possible, to the next Gang in each direction, from which a Platelayer must, in like manner, be sent to the next more distant Gang, until information of the accident has, by this means, reached the nearest Station in

Summoning assistance.

each direction, and the necessary assistance has been obtained; the Platelayers of each Gang proceeding without loss of time to the place at which their services are required.

Articles a Foreman, Ganger, or Leading Man to have when examining Road.

259. Each Foreman, Ganger, or Leading Man, when examining his length of Line, must have with him a Keying Hammer, six Detonators and a Red Flag, a few Key Packings, a Permanent-way gauge, and a Spanner, and when passing through a Tunnel he must also carry a Lighted Hand Signal Lamp.

Foreman, Ganger, or Leading man to walk over his length of Line.

260. (*a*) Each Foreman, Ganger, or Leading Man must walk over his length of Line every morning and evening on week-days, and, where Passenger trains are run, once on Sundays, and tighten up all Keys and other Fastenings that may be loose; and he must examine the Line, Level, and Gauge of the road, and the state of the Joints, marking, and, if necessary, repairing, such as are defective.

NOTE.—*On the Great Western Railway the length may be walked once daily by the Ganger and once by the Leading Packer; and on certain Branch Lines the length may be walked once only, by the Ganger; the special authority of the Divisional Engineer being required in each case.*

Points and Crossings to be examined.

(*b*) All points and crossings must be carefully examined, and, if necessary, adjusted.

Cleaning of Points and Signals.

(*c*) Gangers must oil and keep clean the working parts of Points and Signals, unless the duty is otherwise specially provided for, and the Points must be kept clear of snow, ice, or other obstruction.

Proper Scotch Blocks to be provided.

(*d*) They must also take care to maintain proper Scotch Blocks on all Sidings requiring them, and must see that at Level Crossings, ballast, stones, snow, ice, or other obstructions are not allowed to accumulate so as to interfere with the running of the trains.

Obstructions not to be allowed to accumulate.

(*e*) Any obstruction to the proper working of the Signals or Signal Wires must be removed, and broken Signal Wires must be temporarily repaired until the regular Signal-repairer can attend to them.

Obstruction to proper working of Signals to be removed. Broken Signal Wires to be repaired.

261. Each Foreman, Ganger, or Leading Man must report to the Inspector of Permanent-way every case in which any Signal is disregarded by an Engine-driver. If any Telegraph Pole is in an unsafe state, or any of the Wires are broken, slack, entangled, or touching each other or any building, they must be made safe and the circumstances reported to the Inspector of Permanent-way. The Foreman, Ganger, or Leading Man must also see that all grass, boughs of trees, ballast, and rubbish are removed from the Telegraph and Signal Wires, and from Point Rods.

Disregard of Signals, and defects of Signal Wires and Telegraph.

262. (*a*) An additional Tail Lamp or a Red Board or a Red Flag by day, or an additional Red Tail Light by night, carried on the last vehicle of a train or on an engine, indicates that a Special train or engine is to follow; and Platelayers are required to look for such Signals on the last vehicle of the train. As, however, Special Trains or engines have frequently to be run without previous notice of any kind, it is necessary at all times to be prepared for such extra trains or engines.

Specials following.

Specials run without notice.

(*b*) The additional Tail Signal will not be carried by preceding trains for Special trains of which previous printed or written notice has been given.

Specials run under notice.

Lifting of Permanent-way.

263. In lifting the Permanent-way no lift must be greater than three inches at once, and then it must be effected in a length of at least twenty yards, in such a manner as not to occasion any sudden change of gradient. When both rails have to be lifted they must be raised equally and at the same time, and the ascent must be made in the direction in which the trains run, great care being taken, where there is a curve, to preserve the super-elevation of the outer rail.

Ballast not to be thrown up.

Rails to be kept clear.

264. Ballast must not be thrown up in the four-foot space more than three inches above rail level, and it must be thrown as much as possible on the outside of each Line, or between the two Lines. The rails must be kept clear of gravel, ballast, or any other material.

No blasting without authority of Engineer.

265. Blasting must not be allowed on any slopes or elsewhere on or near to the Railway without the authority of the Engineer.

Gates to be closed and fastened.

266. Gangers must close and fasten any Gates they find open, and report the circumstances, in order that the persons who are required to keep such Gates closed and fastened may be charged with the penalties.

Examination of Works in case of flood.

267. Each Foreman or Ganger is required, in the event of a flood, to examine carefully the action of the water through the culverts and bridges on his length of Line; and should he see any cause to apprehend danger to the Works, he must immediately exhibit the proper Signals for the trains to proceed cautiously or to stop, as necessity may require, and inform the Inspector thereof; and until the Inspector arrives, he must take all the precautionary measures necessary for securing the stability of the Line.

268. In the event of any fire occurring upon or near the Line, the men employed on the Line must take immediate measures for putting it out.

Fire upon or near the Line.

269. Each Foreman or Ganger must keep his portion of the Line clear and safe, and the fences in perfect repair; and, in the event of any sheep, cattle, or other animals getting within the fences, he must immediately remove them, and report the circumstance to the Inspector of Permanent-way.

Line to be kept clear and safe. Fences to be repaired. Cattle on Line.

270. (*a*) Foremen or Gangers must see that broken chairs, rails, sleepers, or other defective materials are removed from the road with the least possible delay, and that sound materials are substituted.

Defects to be immediately repaired.

(*b*) All cases of broken rails must be specially reported to the Inspector of Permanent-way.

(*c*) Tools, rails, sleepers, pieces of iron or wood, or other implement or material, must be carefully placed so as to be quite clear of the Line, and not within two feet of the rails, and the disused materials must be removed from the Line as soon as practicable.

Implements and materials to be kept clear of rails, and materials to be removed as soon as practicable.

271. Each Inspector of Permanent-way is held responsible for the security of rails, chairs, and sleepers, and other Permanent-way materials in his district, and for their being kept clear of both Lines, and properly stacked.

Responsibility for security of rails, chairs and other materials.

Security of tools and implements.

272. Tools and implements required for the repair of the Line must, when not in use, be kept locked up in a building, or in boxes, for the security of which each Foreman or Ganger on his own length of Line is responsible.

Men to keep clear of trains.

273. (*a*) When a train is approaching, Platelayers and other men at work on the Permanent-way must not remain on any Running Lines, nor between them if the spaces are less than eight feet, but must at once move clear of all Lines, unless they can distinctly see that they are in a position of safety, and in no danger from another train approaching them unobserved; the men must stop in the positions they have taken up till the train has cleared a sufficient distance to enable them to see that no train is approaching on the other Lines before they recross the rails.

(*b*) If circumstances compel Platelayers or other men to remain in the six-feet space between trains passing on adjoining Lines, they must lie down.

Flagman to be appointed.

(*c*) In Tunnels or where the approach of a train cannot be observed or heard in time for the men to get out of the way, a Flagman or other competent person must be appointed by the Ganger to give the necessary warning. On Single Lines the working party must be protected in both directions.

Men to desist from work during fog or falling snow.

(*d*) The men must also desist from work in cases of fog or falling snow when the Foreman, Ganger, or Leading Man considers that they would not have sufficient warning of the approach of a train, provided such discontinuance of work does not endanger the safety of the trains.

(*e*) Where of necessity a Gang of men is working in a fog or during falling snow, the Foreman, Ganger, or Leading Man in charge must send out a man in each direction to warn the Gang of the approach of a train, either by shouting or using a fog-horn or loud whistle, and, if the occasion require it, the men sent out must place a Detonator on one rail of the Line on which the train is approaching.

Warning men at work.

(*f*) When men are working singly or in gangs on or near lines in use for traffic for the purpose of relaying or repairing the Permanent-way of such lines, the Foreman, Ganger, or Leading Man must, in all cases where any danger is likely to arise, provide one or more persons, as may be necessary, to maintain a good Look-out, and to give warning of any train approaching. The "Look-out" man or men must be expressly instructed to act for such purpose, and must be provided with all appliances necessary to give effect to such "Look-out."

Protection of Gangs.

NOTE.—*Where an authorised apparatus is provided for the purpose of giving warning, it will not be necessary to employ "Look-out" men.*

274. When a Ballast train has to be moved whilst men are in the trucks the Foreman, Ganger, or Leading Man must warn the men, and the Engine-driver must sound his Whistle, before the waggons are moved. The Engine-driver must also sound his Whistle before reducing the speed preparatory to stopping.

When Ballast train has to be moved whilst men are in trucks.

275. (*a*) Men working in a Tunnel, when trains are approaching in both directions, must

Working in Tunnels.

if unable to reach any recess in the walls, lie down either in the space between the two Running Lines, or between the Line and the side of the Tunnel, until the trains have passed. The width of the space depends upon the construction of the Tunnel, with which every man must make himself acquainted, in order that he may select the place which affords the greatest safety.

Drivers to whistle on entering and passing through Tunnels.

Drivers not to throw out hot water, &c., in Tunnel.

Breach of Rule to be reported.

(*b*) Engine-drivers have instructions that the Whistle must be sounded on entering a Tunnel to warn all men who are working inside, and that it must be repeated occasionally when passing through long Tunnels, and they also have instructions not to throw out hot water, fire, or cinders whilst passing through a Tunnel; any omission to comply with these instructions must be reported by the Foreman, Ganger, or Leading Man to his Inspector.

Materials found on Line to be collected.

276. Each Foreman, Ganger, or Leading Man is responsible for collecting any coupling, chains, hooks, pins, iron, or other materials found on the Line, and for having them conveyed to the nearest Station as early as practicable.

Luggage and goods found on Line to be taken to nearest Station.

277. Luggage, goods, or other articles, not referred to in the preceding Rule, found on the Line must immediately be taken to the nearest Station-master, and a report made containing the best information that can be obtained respecting the train from which they may have fallen

Company's workmen not to travel with passengers.

278. Platelayers and other workmen of the Company holding third-class passes must ride in a third-class carriage, and, when possible, in a compartment by themselves separate from passengers. When a large number of workmen travel by the same train carriages will be provided for their use, and they must ride in these carriages only.

CONVEYANCE BY GOODS TRAINS OF EXPLOSIVES AND DANGEROUS GOODS.

279. The following Code of Instructions must be observed by Guards and others with respect to the conveyance of Vehicles containing Explosives and other Dangerous Goods :—

Instructions respecting Explosives, &c.

1. While the loading, unloading, or conveyance of Explosives or other Dangerous Goods is going on, each person engaged in such loading, unloading, or conveyance must observe all necessary precautions for the prevention of accident by fire or explosion; must not allow any unauthorised person to have access to such goods; must abstain from smoking or any act whatever which tends to cause fire or explosion, and is not reasonably necessary for the loading, unloading, or conveyance; and must prevent any other person from committing any such act. Further, he must not have upon him any matches.

2. Inflammable Liquids, Oily Rags, Oily Waste, Oily Paper, Oily Canvas, Oily Mill Sweepings, and similar goods, must be loaded in separate waggons (iron-bottomed waggons being used in all cases when available), which must be kept as far away as practicable from

others containing goods, and such waggons must not be placed within the Company's Sheds or Warehouses.

3. In loading or unloading any Explosive, the casks and packages containing the same must, as far as practicable, be passed from hand to hand, and not rolled upon the ground, and in no case must any such casks or packages be rolled unless clean hides, cloths, or sheets have been previously laid down on the platform or ground over which the same are to be rolled. Casks or packages containing Explosives must not be thrown or dropped, but must be carefully deposited and stowed.

4. Gunpowder Vans must in every case be locked when sent loaded with Gunpowder, and the key forwarded to the receiving station.

5. Distinctive labels are provided, and on no account must vehicles containing Explosives or other Dangerous Goods, except when in metallic cases or cylinders, be allowed to travel unless one of these is securely affixed on each side, in order that the Guards may be aware of the contents.

6. Whenever vehicles containing Explosives, Inflammable Liquids, or other Dangerous Goods have to be forwarded by train, the special attention of the Head Guard in charge of the train must be called to the vehicles by a duly authorised person, and he will be held responsible for the

proper observance of these instructions while the goods are being conveyed on the train, and until they are delivered into the safe custody of the Station Staff.

7. The vehicles must be placed as far as practicable from the engine, and no fire must be allowed in the Guards' Break-vans when any vehicles containing such goods are attached to the train, and not more than five vehicles containing Explosives must be conveyed by any one train at any one time.

8. Vehicles containing Oil or other traffic of an inflammable nature must not be put on the train near to vehicles containing Gunpowder or other Explosive.

9. At every Station at which a train stops the Guard in charge must make a special examination of the waggons containing any description of Explosives or other Dangerous Goods, and must more especially examine the axle-boxes, and, if the axles show the least sign of heating, the waggon must be detached, and the attention of the Agent or Foreman specially directed to it. *Special care must be taken not to bring any light in close proximity to waggons containing Explosive or Inflammable Goods.*

In the event of it being necessary to detach, as unfit to travel, any such vehicle at any point short of its destination, the Guard must advise the person in charge of the Station or Siding where the vehicle is detached, in order that the necessary precautions may be taken by all concerned in dealing with the defective vehicle.

10. Gunpowder for Branch Stations, or for any Station not on the direct route to be taken by the van, must not be sent in small lots requiring transhipment, except it be packed in metallic cylinders, and when Gunpowder requiring transhipment arrives at a Junction, the transhipment must be effected as speedily as possible.

11. Before detaching at the end of his journey, or at exchange Sidings, vehicles containing any description of Explosives or Dangerous Goods, the Head Guard in charge of the train must call the special attention of a duly authorised person, and obtain his instructions as to the disposal of the vehicles.

12. The waggons must, at the Receiving Station, be immediately separated from other waggons, and at both the Sending and Receiving Stations must not be allowed to come within any of the Company's enclosed Sheds or Warehouses.

NOTES.—*Explosives and other Dangerous Goods must not, except where special instructions are given to the contrary, be carried by trains conveying passengers.*

Loose shunting of vehicles containing Explosives is strictly prohibited.

UNIFORM TIME TO BE KEPT BY GUARDS, AND AT ALL STATIONS.

280. (*a*) Greenwich time, which is adopted throughout all the Railways in Great Britain, will be sent to the principal Stations daily, by telegraph, in accordance with the special instructions on the subject

Greenwich time sent daily.

(*b*) Station masters and Signalmen will be held responsible for keeping their Clocks properly regulated, and must, if necessary, at once report any defects in their working, in order that steps may be taken for their immediate repair.

Clocks to be regulated.

NOTE.—*Block Signal-boxes not provided with Speaking Instruments will be supplied with the time in accordance with Block Telegraph Regulations.*

281. In order to ensure uniform time being kept at all the Stations on the Line to which time is not telegraphed, the following instructions must be observed:—

Instructions to ensure uniform time.

(i.) Each Guard must, before starting on his journey, satisfy himself that his Watch is correct with the Clock at the Station from which he starts, and must again compare it with, and, if necessary, regulate it by, the Clock at the Station where his journey ends, before commencing his return journey.

(ii.) The Station-master or person in charge must obtain the precise time from the Guard in charge of the first stopping Passenger train commencing its journey after 10 a.m., and, in the event of the time given by the Guard differing from that of the Station Clock, the latter must be altered to agree, and regulated accordingly.

This edition published 1993
by Ian Allen Ltd

ISBN 0 7110 2259 3

Printed and bound in Great Britain by
Mackays of Chatham PLC, Chatham, Kent